Crash Test Dummies

WHEN GOD'S PEOPLE KEEP CRASHING INTO THE WALL

CRASH TEST DUMMIES

SURPRISING LESSONS FROM THE BOOK OF JUDGES

TALBOT DAVIS

Abingdon Press / Nashville

Crash Test Dummies
Surprising Lessons from the Book of Judges

Copyright © 2017 Abingdon Press
All rights reserved.

This book is printed on elemental chlorine-free paper.
ISBN 978-1-5018-47561

17 18 19 20 21 22 23 24 25 26—10 9 8 7 6 5 4 3 2 1
MANUFACTURED IN THE UNITED STATES OF AMERICA

CONTENTS

Introduction: Crash Test Dummies .7

1. Last Things First 11

2. The Iron Lady 27

3. Gideon: More than a Hotel Bible 43

4. Appearances Can Be Deceiving 59

5. Déjà Vu All Over Again. 75

6. The Gap Years 93

Notes. 109

Introduction

CRASH TEST DUMMIES

You've seen them, haven't you? They ride in the front seats of expensive cars and drive headlong into brick walls. And then they do it again. Different car, same wall. And again. Different car, same wall. They're crash test dummies.

Why do they keep doing the same dumb thing over and over again? Why do we?

In my quarter-century plus as a pastor, that question has troubled me more than any other: why do people repeat the same mistakes time and time again? Why do they fall into the same self-destructive patterns, get caught up in the same dysfunctions, and become mired in the same behavioral loops and relational traps?

As they say in the corporate world, *"the best predictor of future behavior is . . . past behavior."* And so it is.

Yet as I have pondered this realization—that so many of us are living, breathing crash test dummies who climb into a new car to rush headlong into the same wall—I have found some encouragement in Scripture.

Because we're not the first crash test dummies. We're not even the most accomplished. I guess you could say we're not even the *dummeriest.*

The Old Testament Book of Judges—a book rarely referenced and even more rarely preached or taught—is at its core a book of cyclical history in which the term *crash test dummies* applies to an entire nation of people. In this instance, it applies to the ancient nation of Israel, the people of God.

Here's what you need to know about Judges. As the story opens, the Hebrews have exited Egypt under the leadership of Moses; they have wandered in the desert for forty years under the watchful eye of Moses and the not-so-watchful eye of Aaron; and they have conquered Canaan under the military command of Joshua. Now, for the first time, they are a people and they have a place. It is approximately 1200 BC and they appear to be primed for success, basking in the blessing of God

And what ensues is chaos. Utter chaos.

Lacking spiritual leadership and central governance, the people quickly descend into a cycle of idolatry, apostasy, slavery, and deliverance. According to Judges, here is the recurring pattern of the people's lives:

1. The Israelites break God's covenant by worshiping other gods.

2. Foreign enemies oppress the Israelites.
3. The Israelites cry out to God for help.
4. God raises up a deliverer (a judge) to save the people.
5. The judge delivers the people and leads them back to the covenant.
6. The people remain faithful to God throughout the judge's lifetime.
7. The judge dies, and the Israelites begin to worship other gods.

Wash. Rinse. Repeat.

Remarkably, the Israelites never learn their lesson, and the conclusion of the book is more depressing than its beginning (more on that in chapter 1).

I have to confess: when I first began to study Judges, there seemed to be so few moments of redemption that I began to give up on uncovering anything helpful. As you'll see in the opening chapter, I briefly wondered if I was the crash test dummy thinking that I could make *Crash Test Dummies* come out of this biblical book.

Yet my despair lifted when I realized in a flash: the book only elevates your spirits when you allow it to expose your flaws. I struggled with Judges when I tried to stand apart from it; I received its blessing when I entered into it and discovered all the ways its mixed-up characters are so much like the guy I see in the mirror. Like it is with so much of Scripture, we're not to judge the fools in the story; we're to identify with them. And only in that identification will we ultimately find liberation.

One more word about Judges, the book. Most of us in the twenty-first century are accustomed to learning and reading history from the perspective of precision. The Civil War lasted from April 1861 to April 1865; World War II began for the USA in December of 1941 and ended in August of 1945. We tell history accurately and sequentially, aligning dates and events in chronological order. The ancient Israelite mind did not always operate with those understandings. Rather than telling history with *precision*, the inspired author of Judges tells it in *patterns*. The cyclical patterns are more important to the author than precise dates or sequences of events. When you realize what he is trying to accomplish—and how—the book opens up in all of its God-breathed glory.

I give you that background because after wrestling with Judges, I now love it. I understand it on its terms, not mine, and in so doing I have been moved by its unforgettable characters. Deborah, Jephthah, Samson, Gideon, and more—all are heroes and anti-heroes, victors and villains, broken yet beautiful. In other words, they are like most of the people reading this book.

I have one other hope for you as you read *Crash Test Dummies*, and it's this. The next time you're tempted to put on your seat belt and drive directly into the same old wall full of the same old sins, resulting in the same old regret, you'll have the spiritual wisdom to step out, disembark, and stride into freedom.

1

LAST THINGS FIRST

In those days there was no king in Israel; each person did
what they thought to be right.

(Judges 21:25)

Perhaps you have heard of the major American novelist John
Irving. (Or maybe you have absolutely no idea who he is.) Whether
you've heard of him or not, he has written several carefully crafted,
multi-layered, and frequently hilarious novels. Many of them were
eventually turned into movies; *The World According to Garp* and
The Cider House Rules are two examples. A third movie, *Simon*

Birch, was based on John Irving's novel *A Prayer for Owen Meany*. Even if you haven't read those books, or any of the others John Irving wrote, perhaps you have seen the movies or at least heard of them. He's a brilliant author whose fiction is at the same time entertaining and compelling.

Here's why I'm telling you about John Irving. He composes his books with a very peculiar process: he writes the last sentence first. Irving figures that if he knows the ending, he can put together the story that leads up to it. Knowing the final words helps him to develop his characters and twist his plots. For instance, here's the last line of *A Prayer for Owen Meany*, which is about a boy with a "wrecked voice" who becomes convinced that God has a destiny for him:

> "O God—please give him back! I shall keep asking You."[1]

Knowing that final line, and the paragraphs leading up to it, enabled Irving to craft the whole story about the boy Owen Meany and his relationship with the narrator—how Owen's life, perspective, and heroic sacrifice led to the narrator's faith in God.

It's an interesting way of writing, isn't it? Last sentence first. Now, I know you're probably thankful for this bit of trivia. You're better prepared for a future English class you might take. And if you ever go on *Jeopardy* and get an "American Authors" category, well, you'll be just a little more confident. And yet, I'm sure you are still wondering, "What in the world does this have to do with things like the Bible, Jesus, God, the Book of Judges, and the first chapter of this book?!" I'm glad you asked because the answer is *everything*.

You see, the Book of Judges, one of the more obscure books in the Old Testament, is a work of patterned history told with a novelist's flair and skill. And it's somewhat like a John Irving novel in that the final sentence sheds clarifying perspective on the whole book. The last sentence helps make sense of the tragic, terrible, and perplexing series of stories found in Judges, especially toward the end. In fact, I can imagine that the unknown author of Judges, operating under the inspiration of the Holy Spirit and laying out material to compile into the book, realized in a flash of inspiration: "Ah! Let me write the last sentence first! Everything else in the book will lead up to that (or down to that)." And so, because that last sentence is so important in the Book of Judges, we are going to begin our study with it. Last things first. Doing so will help us get a perspective on the whole book, to set the stage for the stories we will study in our remaining chapters.

So what is it? What is this final sentence that is the lens through which everything else in Judges makes sense? "In those days there was no king in Israel; each person did what they thought to be right" (Judges 21:25). Or as another translation reads, "all the people did what was right in their own eyes" (NRSV).

"IN THOSE DAYS THERE WAS NO KING IN ISRAEL; EACH PERSON DID WHAT THEY THOUGHT TO BE RIGHT." (JUDGES 21:25)

Everything in the Book of Judges has been arranged in such a way that you arrive at the end and encounter the statement "each person did what they thought to be right." This statement also appears in Judges 17:6, so it actually bookends the final five chapters of Judges. These chapters paint a clear picture of chaos, anarchy, and violence. In other words, in the last five chapters of Judges, we see everybody inventing their own individual version of morality, and bedlam is the result. It's one of the unhappiest endings in the entire library of Scripture. And the rest of the book before that is not much better. The Israelites in Judges are like crash test dummies who, for twenty-one chapters, have been doing the same dumb things over and over. And now, in the final chapters, they arrive at a place where they are the dumbest. What a delightful way for us to begin!

Just what were these dumb things? We won't survey the whole book now—there's plenty of opportunity to do that in the chapters that follow—but here's the story behind the story. It's a period of ancient Israelite history when they have just begun to emerge as a people in the land of Canaan. It takes place between about 1200 and 1050 BC. The Israelites have come out of Egypt, wandered in the wilderness, and begun to conquer the Promised Land under Joshua's leadership. Now Joshua has died, and the people are residing in the land as a confederation of tribes and local groups without centralized leadership over all of Israel. This is highlighted by the repeated phrase, "In those days there was no king in Israel" (Judges 17:6; 18:1; 19:1; 21:25). In many ways, the picture of this era in Judges resembles the Wild West of the United States: a lawless frontier, a weak central government, and only the strong—or the clever—survive.

Judges attributes this lawlessness to the Israelites' relentless tendency to worship other gods. God's people, the Israelites, have created this chaotic world for themselves after the deaths of Moses and Joshua by refusing to follow God's laws and seeking other deities. They break their covenant with God over and over again. What results is a pattern that repeats itself throughout the book, an ongoing cycle of sin, oppression, deliverance, and falling right back into sin. Here is the pattern:

1. The Israelites break God's covenant by worshiping other gods.
2. Foreign enemies oppress the Israelites.

3. The Israelites cry out to God for help.
4. God raises up a deliverer (a judge) to save the people.
5. The judge delivers the people and leads them back to the covenant.
6. The people remain faithful to God throughout the judge's lifetime.
7. The judge dies, and the Israelites begin to worship other gods.

And so the cycle repeats itself. We see this pattern in the many stories of the leaders in the Book of Judges—it's the framework that holds the stories together. There is even a short description of the whole pattern near the beginning of the book:

> [11]Then the Israelites did things that the LORD saw as evil: They served the Baals; [12]and they went away from the LORD, their ancestors' God, who had brought them out of the land of Egypt. They went after other gods from among the surrounding peoples, they worshipped them, and they angered the LORD. [13]They went away from the LORD and served Baal and the Astartes. [14]So the LORD became angry with Israel, and he handed them over to raiders who plundered them. He let them be defeated by their enemies around them, so that they were no longer able to stand up to them. [15]Whenever the Israelites marched out, the LORD's power worked against them, just as the LORD had warned them. And they were very distressed.
>
> [16]Then the LORD raised up leaders to rescue them from the power of these raiders. [17]But they wouldn't even obey their own leaders because they were unfaithful, following other gods and worshipping them. They quickly deviated from the way of their ancestors, who had obeyed the LORD's commands, and didn't follow their example.

[18]The LORD was moved by Israel's groaning under those who oppressed and crushed them. So the LORD would raise up leaders for them, and the LORD would be with the leader, and he would rescue Israel from the power of their enemies as long as that leader lived.

[19]But then when the leader died, they would once again act in ways that weren't as good as their ancestors', going after other gods, to serve them and to worship them. They wouldn't drop their bad practices or hardheaded ways.

(Judges 2:11-19)

The cycle of sin, oppression, deliverance, and right back into sin occurs over and over and over. Even the few characters in this book we've been *conditioned* to think are heroes—like Gideon and Samson—aren't all that heroic. When we read their stories in Judges, we find deeply flawed individuals with dramatic downfalls. And as Judges moves from beginning to end, we find things getting worse. Everything spins out of control. Throughout the twenty-one chapters, the cycles become more characterized by sin, violence, and people following their own morality. The crash test dummies get dumber. And it reaches its apex—or rock bottom—in Judges 21.

It comes at the end of a bizarre and grotesque series of events that spans Judges 19–21. You're welcome to read these chapters on your own, though I don't recommend reading them with young children for family devotions. To summarize briefly, a Levite's concubine runs away from his home, and he travels to her father's house to bring her back. On the journey home, the two of them stop in a town called Gibeah, where the men of the town attempt to rape the Levite. Though his host offers protection, the Levite sees that things are getting dangerous, so he sends his concubine out to the men. They rape and abuse her all night, and she dies. The next day the Levite takes her home, dismembers her body, and sends the parts to the Israelite tribes, calling them to war and revenge. The Israelites attack the city of Gibeah, but the people of Benjamin—one of the tribes of Israel—come to the city's defense because it's in their territory. The result is a civil war, in which the Israelites defeat the tribe of Benjamin and kill almost all of its men. There are only a few hundred survivors out of the whole tribe.

At the end of this civil war, the people of Israel are shocked. It's as if they have collective PTSD, civil war style. They have won, but they have also wiped out an entire tribe of their own people. They are victims and villains. Sinners and saints. Liars and misfits. Warriors and warred upon. And they have a change of heart.

They realize that one of their tribes, Benjamin, is now lacking in women because of the civil war. Never mind that this is because they've massacred all the Benjaminites, including women, children, and even animals, going so far as to burn down "every city they came across" (Judges 20:48). For the ancient Israelites, having no women available to be wives for the men (the few that are left of the tribe of Benjamin) meant that tribe would die out. There would be no child-bearing, and therefore no future. And what's more, all the Israelites had vowed not to give their daughters as wives for the Benjaminites (Judges 21:1). The Israelites are suddenly concerned that the whole tribe of Benjamin might cease to exist as a result of their violence and rash vow.

And in the aftermath of that nobody-wins civil war, they ask this question of God at the beginning of Judges 21: "'LORD, God of Israel,' they said, 'why has this happened among us that as of today one tribe will be missing from Israel?' And the next day, the people got up early and built an altar there. They offered entirely burned offerings and well-being sacrifices" (Judges 21:3-4).

The people turn to God to ask why this terrible thing has happened, when in reality, their own actions have brought it all about. The men of Gibeah acted wickedly; the Levite sent his concubine right out to them with no regard for her well-being; and the Israelites sought revenge. It escalated into an all-against-one civil war. And the people turn to God wondering why it all came about. Ha! Do you see the faulty logic and the deep irony? It's like the parents who were teaching their five-year-old about God.

"Who made the sun?" they asked.

"God," said the boy.

"Who made the rain?"

"God," said the boy.

"Who made you?"

"God," said the boy.

Right every time! A few days later, the mom walks into the boy's room and it's a disaster. So she asks, "Who made this mess?"

And without missing a beat, the boy says, "God."

That's what we do so often, isn't it? "Lord, why have you done this to me?" we ask, when deep down we know good and well that we did it to ourselves. Our own actions bring about bad results, and we turn to God as if it were somehow God's fault.

In Judges 21, God does not answer the Israelites' question. They raise up their voices and cry out before God "until evening" (Judges 21:2), and then the next day they get up early, build an altar, and offer sacrifices. And yet Scripture records no response from God at this point. God's silence in the wake of all their pleading is deafening. The silence is God's way of thundering, "You got into this mess all by yourselves." God didn't get the Israelites into a civil war and slaughter of an entire tribe. The people brought it about entirely on their own.

Once I spoke with a man who was having an extramarital affair. He wanted it to end, and he had been praying continuously for the Lord to get him out of it. He'd just kept praying for that, he told me, and he lamented that he'd received no answer from God. I remember thinking to myself, "Well, did you pray that God would get you into the affair in the first place?" Something tells me the guy found his way there all by his lonesome. And the same silence greeted his laments as that which greeted the Israelites in Judges 21.

Do you blame God—or Satan, or some other force beyond your control—for the messes you've made? Perhaps it's a mess with your money, or with your family, or with your church, or in some other area of your life. Do you blame God or something else for it? What would it mean to acknowledge and bear your own responsibility for things? Might God's silence be a challenge to you to accept your role in what's happened and begin to make changes for the better?

WHAT WOULD IT MEAN TO ACKNOWLEDGE AND BEAR YOUR OWN RESPONSIBILITY FOR THINGS?

The Israelites don't make such a response. Instead, in the wake of that silence from God, they invent their way into a whole new kind of morality. They make up the rules as they go. They discover that one city, Jabesh-gilead, did not send any men to fight against the tribe of Benjamin. So they send warriors to attack Jabesh-gilead and kill all the men, children, and women who have slept with a man. They spare only the young women who have not yet slept with a man, so that they can give these to the remaining men of Benjamin as wives (Judges 21:7-14).

The violence continues. Confronted with God's silence, the people start to act in a way that seems right to them. But there's no real change. They just continue doing the very thing that got them there in the first place, attacking one of their own cities and killing most of its people. They use more bloodshed to try to right the wrong done by previous bloodshed. They are inventing their own morality, making up the rules as they go, and the result is violence on top of violence.

And it goes on. Four hundred women are captured from Jabesh-gilead to be wives for the Benjaminites, but that isn't enough for each man to have a wife (Judges 21:12-14). So the Israelites come up with a second plan. There is a big religious festival coming up—think of something like a religious Woodstock or Bonnaroo—and they know there will be large numbers of females from all twelve tribes. So here's what they decide:

> [16]The community elders said, "What can we do to provide wives for the ones who are left, seeing that the Benjaminite women have been destroyed? [17]There must be a surviving line for those who remain from Benjamin," they continued, "so that a tribe won't be erased from Israel. [18]But we can't allow our daughters to marry them, for we Israelites have made this pledge: 'Let anyone who provides a wife for Benjamin be cursed!' [19]However," they said, "the annual festival of the LORD is under way in Shiloh, which is north of Bethel, east of the main road that goes up from Bethel to Shechem, and south of Lebonah." [20]So they instructed the Benjaminites, "Go and hide like an ambush in the vineyards [21]and watch. At the moment the women of Shiloh come out to participate in the dances, rush out from the vineyards. Each one of you, capture a wife for yourself from the women of Shiloh and go back to the land of Benjamin. [22]When their fathers or brothers come to us to object, we'll tell them, 'Do us a favor for their sake.

We didn't capture enough women for every man during the battle, and this way you are not guilty because you didn't give them anything willingly." [23] And that is what the Benjaminites did. They took wives for their whole group from the dancers whom they abducted. They returned to their territory, rebuilt the cities, and lived in them.

(Judges 21:16-23)

Wait, wait, wait. WAIT, WAIT, WAIT! You know what that is? Kidnapping! Rape! Human trafficking! This is the very kind of thing that Good Shepherd Church, where I serve, has taken such an incredible, generous stand against for the last decade or so. The Israelites refuse to break their vow to provide wives for the men of Benjamin, but they have no qualms about sanctioning kidnapping and rape to try to remedy the situation. The Israelites twist their morality, shaping it according to their own whims to justify and endorse this gruesome act of wickedness.

That's the type of thing crash test dummies do. They invent new morality, new meanings or applications for their sacred traditions (like a holy war or a religious festival) in order to justify what they are already doing or what they desperately want to do. A modern example is in the case of American slavery and Jim Crow laws, as people absurdly used the curse of Canaan in Genesis 9:25-27 to justify slavery, racism, and lynching. More recently, we see people inventing all sorts of new interpretations of Scripture and tradition to justify what they want to do in the realm of their own sexual practices.

Crash test dummies that they are, the Israelites disregard law, undermine tradition, and dishonor and violate women. They sanction killing, kidnapping, rape, and human trafficking. And in the perversity of all perversities, they call this good. It's no wonder

21

the author of Judges just decides to end it right here, with the sentence "In those days there was no king in Israel; each person did what they thought to be right" (Judges 21:25). It's like he throws his hands up in exasperation as if to say, "I got nothing. I'm spent. I'm done. When you're in charge, you're out of control." What the Israelites invent is perverted, sick, and predatory, and yet they have the nerve to call it holy. In their eyes, it is right, and it is aligned with God's will. The people have long since abandoned the faith and covenant they had inherited, and they turn now to what they have invented. And disaster is the result. Crash test dummies indeed.

The sad fact is, not much has changed. We today are so quick to turn away from what we inherit and make up our own morality as we go. What we invent is immediate and easy, and it serves our self-interest. We rationalize and justify it so we can do our own thing—what seems right to us—and we get so out of control that we come to believe our own lies. Lies like: "I'm in love with that person." "It felt right." "I deserve it." "It's my money." "They deserved to be the object of gossip." "Those people are so different from me, so they must be inferior." "My anger and hatred are justified." "It doesn't really matter what I believe as long as I'm a good person." In your life, in my life, in the life of a church, even in the life of a nation . . . when you abandon what you've inherited in favor of what you invent, there is no cohesion and only chaos.

That's what we see throughout the Book of Judges, the truth that the author's final sentence brings home in a subtle yet compelling way. Whenever the Israelites worship God and remain faithful to their covenant—when they cling to what they've inherited—they experience life and well-being. Yet time and time again, whenever they reject what they've inherited and invent religion and morality for themselves, disaster ensues. And here at the end, it all spirals out of control. Each person does what he or she thinks is right, and what seems right involves endless violence and treating women as less than chattel.

WHAT YOU INVENT WILL LET YOU DOWN. WHAT YOU INHERIT WILL FREE YOU UP.

When it comes to morality, faith, what we teach, and maybe more than anything, how we make decisions, here's the truth that the end of Judges demonstrates: *What you invent will let you down. What you inherit will free you up.* Don't just do what is right in your own eyes. In most cases, if we're honest, we have already been told what is right and good and true. God's revelation surpasses our intuition. Every time! The reason the Israelites acted like crash test dummies, slamming into walls with the same bad results every time, is that they thought they knew better than God. In the Book of Judges, they never learned. Do you, consciously or subconsciously, believe you are smarter than God? You have a chance to learn, to grow, to commit to what you've inherited and stop inventing morality for yourself, doing only what's right in your own eyes. Every time I get myself into trouble it's because of what I invented. Every time I receive a blessing it's because I line up with what I've inherited.

Not long ago, I was in a denominational meeting when someone said with confidence, "we need to move beyond atonement theory." Which is a way of saying, "we need to admit we're a little *too smart* to need the cross anymore." Such. Baloney. (I could use another phrase starting with *B* and including an *S*.) But I tell you that because only three days later, I attended an event in Charlotte involving churches of various denominations from all over the city. You know what we started with? We began by singing

23

the hymn "Nothing but the Blood."[2] What a powerful witness to the great truth that we inherit: nothing but the blood of Jesus, which we trust with our very lives. Heaven forbid that we ever become so sophisticated that we believe we need to invent anything else. *What you invent will let you down. What you inherit will free you up.*

The blood still works. The cross still applies. The biblical library still has authority. Good Shepherd Church is a modern place, but really, we are all about old-time religion. We don't invent anything but recommit ourselves time and time again to the living relationship with Jesus Christ that we have inherited. The Book of Judges, indeed the whole of Scripture, beckons you to do the same.

Questions for Reflection and Discussion

1. How familiar are you with the Book of Judges? How does the reflection above change your understanding of the book?

2. What are some dumb things you keep doing over and over and over? What is the reason for such repetition in your life?

3. The reflection above suggests that the last line of Judges is a key line for understanding the whole book. In what ways do people today do what they think is right? In business? In government? In faith?

4. What are the dangers of inventing and following our own morality in each of these areas? Why are we tempted to do so?

5. When have you been tempted to invent a "morality of the moment"? What was the result if you followed through on your invention?

6. What does it mean to inherit faith from our predecessors and ancestors rather than inventing something new from conventional wisdom?

7. What room or freedom do we have to explore new things in our faith, such as a word of guidance from the Holy Spirit? How do we know if this comes from God? How can we be sure it's not our own invention?

8. When have you been set free by the wisdom or faith you have inherited?

Focus for the Week

Make a list of the richest treasures of the Christian faith that you have inherited. Throughout the coming week, read through the list each day and ask how this treasured inheritance can shape your decisions, actions, and attitudes.

Prayer

Lord God, I believe in you, God Almighty, who made heaven and earth. I believe in you, Jesus Christ the Son, my Lord, who was conceived by the Holy Spirit, born of the Virgin Mary, and crucified under Pontius Pilate. I believe in you, Jesus, who rose from the dead and now sits at the right hand of God. I believe in you, Holy Spirit. I thank you, Triune God, for the universal church, the communion of saints, the forgiveness of sins, and the hope of resurrection and eternal life. Thank you for the faith I have inherited, which sets me free.[3]

Daily Scripture Readings

Monday: Exodus 20
Tuesday: Matthew 6:9-13
Wednesday: Deuteronomy 6:4-9
Thursday: Matthew 5:1-12
Friday: Luke 10:25-37

2

THE IRON LADY

"Get up! This is the day that the LORD has handed Sisera over to you. Hasn't the LORD gone out before you?"

(Judges 4:14)

I once heard of a man who was very tall but not very athletic. After a while, he got tired of people he met always asking him the same two questions: First, "How's the weather up there?" And second, "Do you play basketball?" The first was an annoying cliché, but that second one really irked him. He wasn't an athlete. No, he didn't play basketball! Finally, one person too many asked him that basketball question, and he'd had enough. And this time, the guy asking the question happened to be a very short man himself. So the tall guy answered, "No. Do you play miniature golf?"

If you've finished laughing (or rolling your eyes), let's consider the phenomenon this joke highlights. It's something we're all familiar with: stereotyping. It's forming a standardized mental picture of a group of people that assumes certain things about them—like assuming a tall person must be a good basketball player. And the truth is, we all do it whether we admit it or not. It might not always be how we think of tall people or short people, but chances are good that there are some groups of people you're guilty of stereotyping.

The word *stereotype* is interesting. Do you know its origin? It's from the world of printing. A stereotype in printing was a metal printing plate which reproduced the same text or image time after time. A stereotype would provide an exact reproduction of the original, saving time and labor on reprint editions because the type wouldn't have to be reset. You could just use the one plate for a page instead of arranging each of the letters again. The stereotype made an exact reproduction. If you saw one page from such a plate, you saw them all. And that's what we do with people when we stereotype them: we think that if we've seen one tall person (or short, or white, or black, or young, or old), we've seen them all.

You know this. You do this. We all do. Sometimes men will make stereotypical comments about women. And sometimes women will return the favor. White people form stereotypes about African Americans, who form their own stereotypes about white people. And of course, it's true for other ethnic groups as well. Older folks will stereotype members of younger generations, especially if they have tattoos and wear their hats crooked. And younger persons give it right back, stereotyping those millions who still haven't figured out Uber. Some people stereotype *me*, because

I'm over fifty and a tech novice in some ways . . . or because I went to college in New Jersey . . . or simply because I'm a preacher. That last one is actually entertaining for me. I love being around people who don't know that I'm a pastor, but then they suddenly find out and their behavior changes. One minute their language is . . . colorful, and the next minute they are perfect angels on the way to church. It's as if they think I'll pass judgment on them in some way, which of course isn't true. But it happens all the time because as a pastor I've been stereotyped as someone who can't handle the truth.

And here's something else a lot of us do: we stereotype ourselves. Mentally, we label ourselves or talk to ourselves as if our current reality is our permanent destiny. For me, it was always, "I'm shy and sarcastic." It meant I adopted a certain attitude, put myself into a certain box, and limited myself. For you, it could be different. Maybe it's "I stink at relationships" or "I was raised racist." Perhaps it's "I don't get along with certain people" or "I'm not that spiritual." Or maybe it's "I'm too old to learn anything new" or "I'm too young to meet this challenge." Whatever shape it takes, the attitude is that if you've seen one "me," you've seen them all. That's the "me" I'll always be. And the truth is, that kind of thinking limits us and defeats us.

All of this talk of stereotypes paves the path for the next story in the Book of Judges: the story of Deborah in Judges 4, which is also the story of other figures named Barak, Sisera, and Jael. It's a story I've rarely read or preached on. It's one I've wrestled with and even despaired over, because it has a perplexing message and a vividly bloody conclusion that I've never known what to do with. I struggled so much with it that, at a leader's meeting a while back, I asked some folks to pray for me as I prepared to write a sermon on it. They prayed for my sermon preparation, and then I got a good night's sleep. And the next morning it was obvious to me what was in the story all along: stereotypes. As we're going to see, God breaks down all the stereotypes surrounding Deborah and those around her, with dramatic and miraculous results.

The Book of Judges is one in which the Israelites behave like crash test dummies: they do the same dumb things over and over again. Just as crash test dummies get in a car and slam into a wall—and keep doing it—the Israelites turn away from God time and time again. And the result is the same disappointing, tragic consequences every time. The Israelites during the period of the judges repeat a pattern of sin, oppression, turning back to God, deliverance, and then returning to sin. In the previous chapter, we saw this general pattern described in Judges 2:11-19. And in each story in Judges, we can see the pattern play out in specific yet predictable ways. However, the story of Deborah shows us how we can break those patterns and find liberation through the power of God. Deborah's story challenges us to allow God to break down stereotypes—our stereotypes of others or our stereotypes of ourselves. When we do that, we can appreciate and experience the mighty things God is able to do in our lives. We'll see that Deborah is without a doubt the smartest of all the crash test dummies.

Judges is set in the time from 1200 to 1050 BC, when Israel was just in its infancy as a people. The Israelites had taken possession of the land, but they had enemies encircling them, and they didn't yet have kings like Saul, David, and Solomon to rule over them. Instead, they had a series of charismatic leaders, rescuers, and prophets who collectively are called judges. Deborah is one such judge, and her story begins in Judges 4:1-3:

> [1]After Ehud had died, the Israelites again did things that the LORD saw as evil. [2]So the LORD gave them over to King Jabin of Canaan, who reigned in Hazor. The commander of his army was Sisera, and he was stationed in Harosheth-ha-goiim. [3]The Israelites cried out to the LORD because

Sisera had nine hundred iron chariots and had oppressed the Israelites cruelly for twenty years.

Ehud, the judge mentioned in verse 1, had saved Israel from the king of Moab (his story is found in Judges 3:12-30). But after Ehud's death, the Israelites again turn away from God (which, given the title of this book, shouldn't surprise you at all). And this time, they find themselves under the dominion of a Canaanite king named Jabin and his general Sisera. Sisera's army is powerful; it boasts nine hundred chariots of iron (4:3). That detail that the chariots were made of iron is telling, because this time period is at the very beginning of the Iron Age of human history. This means Jabin and Sisera have the most advanced technology of their day, cutting-edge weaponry. In other words, they are unbeatable. They have a large, professionally staffed, superbly equipped army. Anything the Israelites will be able to muster against them, by comparison, might as well be made in the neighbor's garage and held together with duct tape. That might not be much of an exaggeration. Judges 5, a poetic account of this same story, says "there wasn't a shield or spear to be seen among forty thousand in Israel" (Judges 5:8).

Verse 3 tells us the Israelites cried out to the Lord because of their suffering for twenty years at the hands of Jabin and Sisera. The next six verses relate the answer to the people's outcry:

4Now Deborah, a prophet, the wife of Lappidoth, was a leader of Israel at that time. 5She would sit under Deborah's palm tree between Ramah and Bethel in the Ephraim highlands, and the Israelites would come to her to settle disputes. 6She sent word to Barak, Abinoam's son, from Kedesh in Naphtali and said to him, "Hasn't the LORD, Israel's God, issued you a command? 'Go and assemble at Mount Tabor, taking ten thousand men from the people of Naphtali and Zebulun with you. [7]I'll lure Sisera, the commander of Jabin's army, to assemble with his chariots and troops against you at the Kishon River, and then I'll help you overpower him.'"

[8]Barak replied to her, "If you'll go with me, I'll go; but if not, I won't go."

[9]Deborah answered, "I'll definitely go with you. However, the path you're taking won't bring honor to you, because the LORD will hand over Sisera to a woman." Then Deborah got up and went with Barak to Kedesh. [10]He summoned Zebulun and Naphtali to Kedesh, and ten thousand men marched out behind him. Deborah marched out with him too.

(Judges 4:4-10)

The Israelites cry out to the Lord in verse 3, and verse 4 introduces a woman named Deborah. Do I need to point out the obvious? She's a woman. And a leader. Often preachers will use this passage to celebrate the role of women in the church, but I find that trivializes not only women in general but Deborah in particular. Her story is so much more interesting than that! Instead, I want to pay attention to the contrast that's embedded right there in the story: iron chariots and a woman leader. We need to recognize the stereotypes that readers bring to this Scripture passage. The Israelite readers of this story naturally would have asked, "What can a nation led by a woman possibly do against a people protected by iron?"

It's not a question of men versus women or Israelite versus foreigner. It's a lady versus iron. And every stereotype says that the lady has no chance. "If you've seen one lady, you've seen them all."

Women are nurturers, not leaders, goes the stereotype. "If you've seen one iron chariot, you've seen them all." Iron chariots are unstoppable destroyers. Except that's not how it plays out. Deborah is the unstoppable one.

As it turns out, Deborah defies all kinds of stereotypes, especially those from 1200 BC. First, she's a prophet, one who speaks for God to her people (Judges 4:4). Prophets were usually male. Deborah is one of only four women in the entire Old Testament who are identified as prophets (see Exodus 15:20; 2 Kings 22:14; and Nehemiah 6:14 for the others). So she had an uncommon level of religious leadership for a woman of her time, which she used to settle disputes among the Israelites. Second, she exercises this leadership by sending word to a man, Barak, with instructions to lead the Israelites in battle (Judges 4:6-7). And third, these instructions are quite bold, as Deborah tells Barak to take ten thousand troops and go fight against Sisera, with his nine hundred chariots of iron. And she gives these instructions in God's name, with divine authority.

Barak, for his part, seems to deny his own manliness in reply. "If you'll go with me, I'll go," he says, "but if not, I won't go" (Judges 4:8). It sounds like he's being a coward, refusing to go without Deborah to accompany him. "I'm not going unless you're with me!" Imagine what it must have looked like for a military commander to refuse to go to battle without a woman there to help him lead.

Yet there's another possibility: perhaps Barak's actual wisdom surpasses any apparent cowardice. It may be that Barak is breaking stereotypes here, too—the stereotypes that say only men lead warriors in battle and women have nothing to contribute. What if Barak sees beyond those stereotypes? He knows that Deborah has the intense God-connection; she's the one who's been chosen to speak for God. So perhaps he decides wisely, regardless of how it looks, that he's not going to go to battle without her. Victory is more important to him than appearances. And it doesn't matter to him that he won't receive honor, that "the LORD will hand over Sisera to a woman" (Judges 4:9), as long as the Israelites win. So maybe Barak's not turning in his man card after all. It could be that he's such a manly man that he's willing to stop and ask for directions from a woman!

Deborah, of course, is only too glad to give those directions. After Barak brings his army up to Mount Tabor, Sisera brings his chariots out to meet him. Then Deborah tells Barak to attack because God has given him the victory: "Get up! This is the day that the LORD has handed Sisera over to you. Hasn't the LORD gone out before you?" (Judges 4:14).

"HASN'T THE LORD GONE OUT BEFORE YOU?"

Everything pivots on that one verse. It's Barak's ten thousand men versus the whole army of Sisera. It's homemade weapons versus iron chariots. It's woman-led soldiers versus Sisera, the great commander. Every expectation, every stereotype, every "if you've seen one, you seen them all" situation says that this will be no contest. But Deborah's words say otherwise: "The LORD has handed Sisera over to you." Barak attacks, and God brings him victory:

> So Barak went down from Mount Tabor with ten thousand men behind him. ¹⁵The LORD threw Sisera and all the chariots and army into a panic before Barak; Sisera himself got down from his chariot and fled on foot. ¹⁶Barak pursued the chariots and the army all the way back to Harosheth-ha-goiim, killing Sisera's entire army with the sword. No one survived.
>
> (Judges 4:14-16)

All those chariots literally are thrown into a panic, and Barak defeats them completely. The poetic account of this story in Judges 5 says that even the stars and the Kishon river fought against Sisera, with God using nature to bring about victory (Judges 5:20-21). Israel wins in a landslide. Every stereotype is crushed. Every expected result is reversed. And it all hinges on Deoborah's boldness in 4:14: "the LORD *has handed*" the victory to Israel before it even happens! Deborah believes before she ever sees.

The victory Deborah and Barak experience invites us to trust boldly in God's power despite stereotypes. When I consider this story with that in mind, it leads me to this perspective: ***God breaks down your stereotypes to build up your boldness.*** We who hear or read the story of Deborah and Barak have stereotypes regarding iron chariots, women leaders, and men soldiers who ask directions . . . and God brings every single one of those stereotypes crashing down. You've seen one you've seen them all? Hardly. Iron isn't unstoppable. Chariots aren't invincible. Women aren't inferior leaders. Men who follow them aren't fools. Deborah, Barak, and the Israelites aren't limited by their stereotypes. Each one of them, like each one of us, is unique, God-designed, and brimming with potential.

GOD BREAKS DOWN YOUR STEREOTYPES TO BUILD UP YOUR BOLDNESS.

This story prompts us to consider how we might move past the limitations our own stereotypes place on us. What stereotypes stand in our way, and how does God call us to be bold in breaking them down? The longer white people regard black people as "seen one seen them all"; the longer black people think of white people as

35

"you know what they are all like"; the more we view others through a cookie-cutter lens of suspicion and predictability, the more our faith is weak and powerless. God desires to rid every one of us of that old, stale, stereotypical thinking in our assessments of other people. God wants to remove those stereotypes so that instead of becoming bitter and prejudicial, we can become full of faith and boldness. *God breaks down your stereotypes to build up your boldness.*

Ultimately, when we stereotype others in the ways we often do, we end up stereotyping God. We assume God can only work in certain, familiar ways. We deny that God can work through people we look down upon. We deny that women can be great leaders; that men can be sensitive; that older people can have exciting new ideas; that younger people can behave with wisdom and sound judgment. When we do so, we deny that God created these people as individuals, and we deny what God is capable of doing through them. Deborah's story is a caution for all of us not to stereotype God, believing we know what God is like and what God will do and whom God will do it through. *God breaks down your stereotypes to build up your boldness.*

Some of us act as if God is enthroned on pipe organs and robes and hymnals, and that God never shows up anywhere else. Others of us act as if an encounter with pen and ink in the Bible is the only way to experience God. And still others think God's accessible only through three praise choruses straight from 1995, no more, no less. It's why we resist new forms of worship, why we feel uncomfortable with unfamiliar songs or rituals. It's why we don't wholly trust that we can encounter God in our neighbor whom we serve. Instead, what would it mean if we could be like Deborah, who says in the face of seemingly insurmountable odds: the Lord has handed victory to you. Hasn't the Lord gone out before you?

When we stereotype others—when we say women are this way, whites are like that, that's what Hispanics do—we limit God. When we stereotype ourselves—when we say I'm a drunk, I have ADD, I'm biblically ignorant—we limit God. And whenever we stereotype God, limit God, the result is simply devastating. We miss out on so much victory, so much blessing, so much divine power, because we don't believe God is great enough to get past our stereotypes. My prayer is that from today forward, we'd all be more like Deborah, trusting in God with boldness and deep faith.

There is a story of a woman whose husband booked a flight on an airplane for the two of them. They were going on a trip out of town, and she was excited about it until she found out they'd be flying on a twin-engine propeller plane.

"I'm not going," she said.

"Why not?" he asked.

"Because I'm not going on that tiny little private plane."

"Honey, your faith is too small," he answered.

"No," she said. "Your plane is too small."

Well, the husband really wanted her to come with him, so he canceled the tiny plane and booked on a major airline. She decided to go with him after all, saying "My faith grew because the size of the plane did."

My hope for all of us is that we'd grow the size of our God. My hope is that we'd stop acting as if God is a twin-engine Cessna with limited resources to bless us, to empower us, to go before us and give us victory. No, God is the jumbo airliner eager for us to give him advance gratitude for the blessings and abundance he wants to shower on us.

This means a lot of us will have to stop listening to the negative self-talk we've been using through the years. We have to look beyond the false limitations we've placed on ourselves—not because we're so good, but because God is so mighty. Some who have stereotyped themselves as drinkers might really just be running from a call into ministry. Others who have labeled themselves with an eating disorder may really be just running from a call to work with children. And still others who think of themselves as poor leaders need to be ministering with teenagers. And there are some who have had failure spoken into their lives from an early age, and that's their self-stereotype. And God wants to break through that so hard that they go and start their own businesses. **God breaks down your stereotypes to build up your boldness.**

Now there's one other stereotype that is crushed in Judges 4. In the aftermath of the battle, where Israel routs the iron-clad Canaanite army, Sisera escapes. The commander of the Canaanites gets away and flees to the tent of a woman named Jael. Jael's husband had signed a peace treaty with Sisera's people (Judges 4:17). So Sisera figures he's running to a safe sanctuary. What follows is one of the most vivid scenes in the Bible:

> [18]Jael went out to meet Sisera and said to him, "Come in, sir, come in here. Don't be afraid." So he went with her into the tent, and she hid him under a blanket.
>
> [19]Sisera said to her, "Please give me a little water to drink. I'm thirsty." So she opened a jug of milk, gave him a drink, and hid him again. [20]Then he said to her, "Stand at the entrance to the tent. That way, if someone comes and asks you, 'Is there a man here?' you can say, 'No.'"
>
> [21]But Jael, Heber's wife, picked up a tent stake and a hammer. While Sisera was sound asleep from exhaustion, she tiptoed to him. She drove the stake through his head and down into the ground, and he died. [22]Just then, Barak

arrived after chasing Sisera. Jael went out to meet him and said, "Come and I'll show you the man you're after." So he went in with her, and there was Sisera, lying dead, with the stake through his head.

(Judges 4:18-22)

This story is violent and disturbing. But why is such a bloody story here? A better question to ask might be, what is the effect of including this story here? There are many, and I can think of one especially powerful effect: to break down the stereotype regarding women and non-Israelites. Jael is a woman, like Deborah, whom the readers expect will be gentle and submissive. Sisera certainly doesn't think he has anything to fear from her when he falls asleep in her tent. And Jael is a non-Israelite, an outsider, the last person in the world you'd expect to help Israel. Yet she breaks both of these stereotypes and acts as Israel's deliverer. She's the foreigner who brings victory. She's the woman who conquers and destroys. She's the stereotype God breaks down. ***God breaks down your stereotypes to build up your boldness.***

And before you go thinking about "poor Sisera," Judges 5 lets us know *from his own mother's mouth* that he was a known rapist. Looking out the window waiting for her son to come home, Sisera's mother surmises that he's just dividing the spoils of war after victory, including "a girl or two for each warrior" (Judges 5:30). That was his spoils of war—the reality of kidnap and rape after battle in the ancient world. So Sisera got some justice in the end. God shatters Sisera's stereotype as indestructible. God breaks apart Jael's stereotype as a meek outsider. And it all happens so we will know that bold, life-altering faith comes when we bring an end to the stereotypes of others, of ourselves, and most of all, of our God. ***God breaks down your stereotypes to build up your boldness.***

The most powerful example of this I've witnessed was from a man at Good Shepherd Church who was raised in a segregationist environment. He'd been raised to believe that racial segregation was the proper order of things. He was a white guy raised to view black people—and himself—through the lens of powerful racial stereotypes. Then Jesus happened to him. God met this man and started breaking down his stereotypes. He eventually went through extended illness and then death, and through that I got to see a lot of his journey out of segregation. At his funeral, I was privileged to be one of the speakers. So was his favorite pastor at Good Shepherd, who was a black man. The Life Group in which this man participated was about fifty percent African American, and they were visiting his family and offering their condolences. We saw in those moments what a dramatic change had come about in this man's life. We saw clear evidence that God had broken down his stereotypes. He had formed deep relationships with people he previously would have ignored, and those connections made a dramatic impact on his life. All of us who saw that changed life before our very eyes were inspired. Our faith soared. *God breaks down your stereotypes to build up your boldness.*

Questions for Reflection and Discussion

1. When have you ever been stereotyped by others? On what basis did they stereotype you? What was your response?

2. How have you stereotyped others? Take a few minutes and think through how your attitudes toward other individuals or groups have been shaped by stereotypes.

3. When has one of your stereotypes been upended and proven wrong? What did you learn from that experience?

4. In what ways do you label, stereotype, or limit yourself?

5. List all of the stereotypes that are at play in the story of Deborah in Judges 4. How does God break down each one?

6. How would you characterize Barak in Judges 4? Is his behavior something to praise, or to criticize? Why?

7. What was the source of Deborah's confidence in God? How was she able to be so bold when she instructed Barak to attack (see Judges 4:14)?

8. What self-stereotypes does this story help you break? What stereotypes (or limitations) of God does it help you break?

9. To what boldness is God calling you right now?

Focus for the Week

Locate someone at work or in your neighborhood or in your church who looks different from you, talks differently from you, or was born in a different nation from the one where you were born. Issue that person an invitation to lunch or to coffee and ask simply, "Where were you born, and what's happened since?"

Prayer

Lord God, we praise you that in accordance with Revelation 7:9, we know that every tribe and tongue and nation and land is surrounding the throne of heaven right now, offering you praise and adoration. Would you give us plenty of practice here on earth so we will be well prepared for what awaits us in heaven? Amen.

Daily Scripture Readings

Monday: 1 Kings 14-15
Tuesday: 1 Kings 16-17
Wednesday: 1 Kings 18-19
Thursday: 1 Kings 20
Friday: 1 Kings 21

3

GIDEON: MORE THAN A HOTEL BIBLE

"You have strength, so go and rescue Israel from the power
of Midian. Am I not personally sending you?"

(Judges 6:14)

We long for a God who will enable us. By *enable* I mean the
phenomenon where people allow, tolerate, support, or underwrite
the misbehavior of others. Enabling is a classic and very real
concept in the world of addiction and recovery. It's behavior that's

usually meant to help, but that actually does harm because it allows the addictive behavior to continue with no pressure to change. Chances are, you know what I'm talking about. Maybe you watch Dr. Phil and are familiar with the phenomenon from that show or another one like it. Or maybe you watch TV dramas that deal with it in artful, powerful ways. Or perhaps you know what I'm talking about because you are in the middle of living it—either as someone who enables another or as someone whom other people enable.

In the language of addiction and recovery, enabling makes the non-addict a codependent with the addict. The addict's problem becomes your problem. Addicts manipulate enablers into perpetuating and fueling their addiction, even to the point of accepting the blame. But enabling, while it includes addictive behavior, actually goes far beyond it. Yes, it's the husband who covers up his wife's drinking, extracting promises of "never again" yet never acting on any consequences. But it's also the parents who keep giving an allowance to their twenty-one-year-old son, despite knowing that he is parked in the basement, hooked on his video games. It's also the wife who endures lie after lie and affair after affair, believing every pitiful apology and then enduring every new agony. It's the abuser who makes his victim actually believe she deserves the abuse, and the victim who buys it. It's the person who keeps taking in her single friend who makes no attempt to restore order to her own life. It's the boss at work who tolerates, who disciplines, who manages around, but who never releases an unqualified or underperforming employee. Enabling includes but is not limited to addiction. It's all around, and it all happens when we enable—allow, tolerate, underwrite—the harmful behavior of someone around us.

Subconsciously or not, enabling is the kind of expectation that many of us bring to our conception of and connection with

God. We long for a God who will enable us. I think of the people who through the years have come into my office asking for healing prayers over their compulsive behavior—usually related to alcohol or pornography. And yet on many occasions, those same supplicants have been strangely unwilling to enter into a Twelve Step program tailored to bring long-term recovery from their struggles. These people, it seems, want God to do *for* them what God longs to do *with* them.

We see this in the Book of Judges, in the story of Gideon. As we discussed in the first chapter, Judges shows us a pattern of sin in which the Israelites repeatedly followed other gods and then turned back to the Lord for deliverance when their faithlessness led to disaster. They acted like crash test dummies, doing the same dumb things over and over and over again. That's essentially what the Book of Judges is: an account of the Israelites' vicious, descending cycle of foolishness and sin during their early history in the Promised Land, from about 1200 to 1050 BC. The cycle leads right up to that retrospective last line: "In those days there was no king in Israel; each person did what they thought to be right" (Judges 21:25). Throughout this cycle, it seems to me that the Israelites wanted God to enable them—to keep showing up and bailing them out while their destructive behavior continued.

Yet in the story of Gideon, which begins in Judges 6, we see a moment in which God refuses simply to enable the Israelites. God wants to do something else. And that something else will come about through a man named Gideon. We're actually going to spend two chapters talking about Gideon, because his story has many layers. It turns out that Gideon is much more than just a familiar name we know from the Bibles that show up in our hotel rooms. Gideon's story runs from Judges 6–8, but for now we're just going to look at the scene where God commissions him, in Judges 6. Here is the story:

¹The Israelites did things that the LORD saw as evil, and the LORD handed them over to the Midianites for seven years. ²The power of the Midianites prevailed over Israel, and because of the Midianites, the Israelites used crevices and caves in the mountains as hidden strongholds. ³Whenever the Israelites planted seeds, the Midianites, Amalekites, and other easterners would invade. ⁴They would set up camp against the Israelites and destroy the land's crops as far as Gaza, leaving nothing to keep Israel alive, not even sheep, oxen, or donkeys. ⁵They would invade with their herds and tents, coming like a swarm of locusts, so that no one could count them or their camels. They came into the land to destroy it. ⁶So Israel became very weak on account of Midian, and the Israelites cried out to the LORD.

⁷This time when the Israelites cried out to the LORD because of Midian, ⁸the LORD sent them a prophet, who said to them, "The LORD, Israel's God, proclaims: I myself brought you up from Egypt, and I led you out of the house of slavery. ⁹I delivered you from the power of the Egyptians and from the power of all your oppressors. I drove them out before you and gave you their land. ¹⁰I told you, 'I am the LORD your God; you must not worship the gods of the Amorites, in whose land you are living.' But you have not obeyed me."

¹¹Then the LORD's messenger came and sat under the oak at Ophrah that belonged to Joash the Abiezrite. His son Gideon was threshing wheat in a winepress to hide it from the Midianites. ¹²The LORD's messenger appeared to him and said, "The LORD is with you, mighty warrior!"

[13]But Gideon replied to him, "With all due respect, my Lord, if the LORD is with us, why has all this happened to us? Where are all his amazing works that our ancestors recounted to us, saying, 'Didn't the LORD bring us up from Egypt?' But now the LORD has abandoned us and allowed Midian to overpower us."

[14]Then the LORD turned to him and said, "You have strength, so go and rescue Israel from the power of Midian. Am I not personally sending you?"

[15]But again Gideon said to him, "With all due respect, my Lord, how can I rescue Israel? My clan is the weakest in Manasseh, and I'm the youngest in my household."

[16]The LORD replied, "Because I'm with you, you'll defeat the Midianites as if they were just one person."

[17]Then Gideon said to him, "If I've gained your approval, please show me a sign that it's really you speaking with me. [18]Don't leave here until I return, bring out my offering, and set it in front of you."

The Lord replied, "I'll stay until you return."

[19]So Gideon went and prepared a young goat and used an ephah of flour for unleavened bread. He put the meat in a basket and the broth in a pot and brought them out to him under the oak and presented them. [20]Then God's messenger said to him, "Take the meat and the unleavened bread and set them on this rock, then pour out the broth." And he did so. [21]The LORD's messenger reached out the

tip of the staff that was in his hand and touched the meat and the unleavened bread. Fire came up from the rock and devoured the meat and the unleavened bread; and the LORD's messenger vanished before his eyes. ²²Then Gideon realized that it had been the LORD's messenger. Gideon exclaimed, "Oh no, LORD God! I have seen the LORD's messenger face-to-face!"

²³But the LORD said to him, "Peace! Don't be afraid! You won't die."

²⁴So Gideon built an altar there to the LORD and called it "The LORD makes peace." It still stands today in Ophrah of the Abiezrites.

(Judges 6:1-24)

The story begins, as many stories in Judges do, with the Israelites forsaking God and disaster ensuing: "The Israelites did things that the LORD saw as evil, and the LORD handed them over to the Midianites for seven years" (Judges 6:1). What's interesting is that Judges 5 is a victory song about the great victory and celebration of Deborah, the smartest crash test dummy of them all, the earthly deliverer whose story we studied in the last chapter. And yet after the euphoria of that song, the next thing we read is the despair of 6:1. It goes to show you that we almost always handle adversity better than prosperity because prosperity makes us trust ourselves. We feel we can make our own rules since we have forged our own success. Which is what the Israelites always tend to do in the lawless, ungovernable era we're talking about.

The result of the Israelites' sin is disaster. As we read in verses 2-5, the Midianites oppressed Israel to the point that the Israelites "used crevices and caves in the mountains as hidden strongholds" (6:2). And not only the Midianites, but the Amalekites too, would invade the land whenever the Israelites planted crops. The enemies would ruin the crops and livestock, ravaging the land.

There's something especially interesting about that description in verses 2-5. At this time, the Midianites were nomads and the Israelites were settlers. Yet in response to Israel's sin—which was always idolatry, always the Lord among the gods instead of the Lord alone above all gods—the roles are reversed. After the invasion, the Israelites have to scramble to find temporary (nomadic) shelter in the mountains, caves, and strongholds, while the Midianites reap the benefits of the planted crops and pastures of livestock. The Israelites are displaced from their permanent homes, while the nomadic Midianites eat the produce they've worked to cultivate. It's a total script flip!

I also love the way the narrator exaggerates the threat of the Midianites, likening them to a swarm of locusts coming on countless camels (Judges 6:5). It's a perfect way to turn drama into melodrama, which is characteristic of—you guessed it—people who want you to enable their harmful behavior. And verse 6 summarizes the Israelite response to this role reversal: "So Israel became very weak on account of Midian, and the Israelites cried out to the LORD."

Now, if you've been reading Judges or listening to it (as the earliest audience would have done), you know the pattern when the people cry out like this: God immediately sends a deliverer, a judge. The pattern is spelled out clearly in Judges 2:11-19, and to this point in the story God has raised up Othniel (3:7-11), Ehud (3:12-30), and Deborah (4–5). The people sin, the people get oppressed, the people cry out, and bam! God sends a deliverer. Only this time it changes; look at 6:7-10a:

⁷This time when the Israelites cried out to the LORD because of Midian, ⁸the LORD sent them a prophet, who said to them, "The LORD, Israel's God, proclaims: I myself brought you up from Egypt, and I led you out of the house of slavery. ⁹I delivered you from the power of the Egyptians and from the power of all your oppressors. I drove them out before you and gave you their land. ¹⁰I told you, 'I am the LORD your God; you must not worship the gods of the Amorites, in whose land you are living.' But you have not obeyed me."

Instead of a judge, God sends a prophet. The prophet is unnamed, and he does not predict the future, but tells the Israelites of the past: all that God had done in delivering them from slavery, the how and the why, the main requirement that they not worship other gods. And then the prophet speaks God's firm words: "But you have not obeyed me" (verse 10).

Mic drop. Rather than deliver the people right away, God sends an indictment. And in that delay is everything you need to know. If God had delivered the people immediately following their outcry, God would have been enabling them. God would have been bailing them out for a fourth time after the same harmful behavior that landed them there before. In the prophet's words, I hear God saying "No, no, no. Why should I answer this prayer when you never acted on the last one I answered?" Because God was with the people so much, God had to depart from them. Because God was for the people so much, God had to be temporarily against them. In order to help them, God had first to withhold help. God here refuses to be codependent. God will not let Israel's problem become God's problem.

Every parent, spouse, sibling, friend, or boss who didn't bail out, who didn't rescue, who didn't loan money, who didn't tolerate poor work performance knows exactly what God was going through. God sent a history lesson instead of an answered prayer, because that's what Israel needed.

GOD SENT A HISTORY LESSON INSTEAD OF AN ANSWERED PRAYER.

In the aftermath of that rebuke and reminder, God calls Gideon. When the angel of the Lord first appears, Gideon is hiding, working under cover because he is scared of the Midianites: "Then the LORD's messenger came and sat under the oak at Ophrah that belonged to Joash the Abiezrite. His son Gideon was threshing wheat in a winepress to hide it from the Midianites" (Judges 6:11). The walls of the winepress were high enough to block Gideon and the wheat from view, meaning that he could thresh his grain without the Midianites knowing about it. In other words, when we first meet Gideon, he is fearful and hiding, just like the rest of the Israelites. That makes the angel's first words to Gideon especially stand out: "The LORD is with you, mighty warrior!" (Judges 6:12).

There's some humor there—a Bible laugh line! Gideon is cowering, hiding, sniveling, and the Lord's messenger calls him a mighty warrior! Then, as if to prove the irony, Gideon responds to the angel with a timid question: "With all due respect, my Lord, if the LORD is with us, why has all this happened to us? Where are all his amazing works that our ancestors recounted to us, saying, 'Didn't the LORD bring us up from Egypt?' But now the LORD has abandoned us and allowed Midian to overpower us" (6:13).

You can almost hear Gideon speaking with the voice of Oliver Twist pleading for more food: "Please sir . . ." Gideon expresses some frustration in the form of two questions: why and where.

Why has all this happened? And where are all the wonders of God that we used to hear about? Why are we living like nomads while the Midianites settle on our land? And where are all the cool things you used to do in the past for your people?

We have asked those questions of God too. Why, God, did you let me get into this mess, this marriage, this financial trouble, this jail cell? Where are all those great miracles you used to do like parting the Red Sea and raising people from the dead? Why am I having such a hard time, and where are you? We have all asked those questions. I know I have, and I bet you have too.

It's important to notice that God doesn't answer either of Gideon's questions. As with the people of Israel who cried out for a deliverer (and God sent a prophet instead), God responds but doesn't address what Gideon is asking about. See, I think the Lord realizes something (because God is smart, after all): sometimes people ask questions not because they want answers, but because they want attention. They want control. They want to elicit a response, to set the stage for what the other party can do and when. If God here were to answer Gideon, God would be enabling him and the rest of Israel. So God doesn't answer. Instead, God says simply: "You have strength, so go and rescue Israel from the power of Midian. Am I not personally sending you?" (6:14).

Whoa! "You have resources within you, Gideon. You have strength." God doesn't need to give Gideon an *answer*. God needs to give him an *assignment*. You know what God does here? I love it. God doesn't enable. God empowers. God helps Gideon see the strength that he already has within himself. Perhaps the greeting of "mighty warrior" wasn't so ironic after all. Maybe that is what God wants Gideon to see.

In response, Gideon—like us, like so many—tries to make God his codependent again. "With all due respect, my Lord," he says, "how can I rescue Israel? My clan is the weakest in Manasseh, and I'm the youngest in my household" (6:15). But now the Lord does respond, promising divine presence as the source of Gideon's strength: "Because I'm with you, you'll defeat the Midianites as if they were just one person" (6:16). God answers with an affirmation of Gideon's ability and God's presence. What it's about is clear: *God refuses to enable, but God is eager to empower.*

GOD REFUSES TO ENABLE, BUT GOD IS EAGER TO EMPOWER.

God will not allow, underwrite, or tolerate your continued harmful behavior, but God will for sure fuel, accelerate, and mobilize your ministry! The delay to Israel's outcry means everything, and the non-answer to Gideon's question means everything more. God doesn't give answers here; God gives assignments. And God's assignment to Gideon caps the deal. God is so secure! God knows what needs to happen, and God will not let the Israelites' complaints or Gideon's questions manipulate him into deviating from the plan to empower Gideon.

God will not be manipulated, which means I have to ask you: do you have a manipulative relationship with God? You know what I mean. It's the kind of relationship in which you only call on God when you are in a fix. There's a constant temptation for us to ask God to help us in our dilemmas without repenting of what it was that got us into those dilemmas in the first place. "Help me!" we cry. And sometimes, through a delay or a struggle, God has to withhold help in order to empower us to grow. It's as if God says to us sometimes, "Stop waiting for the next answered prayer and start acting on the last one." *God refuses to enable, but God is eager to empower.*

It's remarkable what God says to Gideon: "You have strength." You already have the resources. That's a powerful word for us, because so often we already have everything we need in order to right the ship and begin to follow God. We already have the resources to live our faith with integrity and to engage in remarkable ministry, if only we will act on them. I believe that's true so firmly that there have been times when I have refused to pray for people. That sounds harsh and mean and not at all pastoral! But I recognized that they were using prayer requests as a way to camouflage the fact that they weren't willing to access the prayers that had already been answered and resources already given. I needed to help them see that they already had strength, saying, "Nope, you got this; stop delaying with prayer and start working with your answers." Along the same lines, I've even stopped counseling people before because the longer they hold on to me (or any counselor), the more they're being held back from true, genuine, authentic healing and wholeness. God doesn't want to enable and prolong bad behavior, and God doesn't want us to be spiritually dependent. God instead wants to empower an army of disciples and apostles.

It's so much like Peter Cartwright, a Methodist preacher in the 1800s. One Sunday as he was preparing to preach, his elders came in and said, "President Andrew Jackson is here today. Don't say anything to upset him! The President is here!" So a bit later that morning, after the opening prayers and hymns, Cartwright stood up and said something to this effect: "I've been told President Andrew Jackson is here. I've also been advised to temper my remarks so as not to offend. Well, here goes: Andrew Jackson will die and go to hell just like everyone else if he does not repent and believe the Gospel." Doh! And in response, Andrew Jackson asked him to dinner. I wish I could have met Peter Cartwright because it's clear he was about telling people what they need to hear to empower life change, not what they wanted to hear that would enable self-destruction. Just like the God we meet in Judges. *God refuses to enable, but God is eager to empower.*

What are you empowered to do? For Gideon, it was defeating the Midianites, which he did. In fact, God used Gideon to bring about an incredible, miraculous victory through only three hundred Israelite soldiers, showing that the victory was through divine presence and not through human might (Judges 7:1-25). As we will see in the next chapter, Gideon's ultimate legacy is more in keeping with the whole downward trend of Judges. But in defeating the Midianites, God empowered Gideon to accomplish a great victory. What is the call and direction of your empowering?

Is God testing your faithfulness with small things in order to prepare you to accomplish something larger?

Is God empowering you simply for sobriety? Or on the other hand, is God empowering you to stop enabling? Is God showing you that you are making possible the behavior in others that is slowly but surely killing you? Is God showing you that their problems don't have to be your problems? When it comes to harmful behavior, sometimes they don't grow out of it. They don't just get better with one more chance, one more bail-out. It takes the pain of withdrawal—like God did!—to force the freedom of awareness.

Or is God empowering you to break the cycle in which you were raised? Yeah, you might have been raised in anger and dysfunction, but now you're given the gift of raising the next generation in faith and in love. We can only break those deeply entrenched cycles when we are empowered by the Chain Breaker.

And here's something God empowers all disciples of Christ to do: inviting. We don't say it enough, but here goes: the invited are to become inviters. All. It takes all people to invite all people into a living relationship with Jesus Christ. It's easy to become codependent on a church or community, and let a few (pastors, professional church leaders) carry the load of inviting for many. But the fact is, God calls and equips all of Jesus' followers to proclaim the good news to others and invite them into a living relationship with Jesus Christ. **God refuses to enable, but God is eager to empower.**

Questions for Reflection and Discussion

1. Recall a time in your work, family, community, or even church where you have tolerated or fueled the misbehavior of others. What was the result? How did the situation resolve?

2. As you look back over your life, have there been times when other people enabled your misbehavior? What did you do about it?

3. Judges 6:7-10 is remarkable because of the way God refuses to answer the plea of the people. What lessons might God be trying to instill in you via unanswered prayer?

4. What two questions does Gideon ask when God's messenger first appears to him (see Judges 6:11-13)? How does the messenger respond to the questions?

5. What prompts you to ask those same kinds of questions of God? What answers do you hope to receive?

6. How does Gideon's story change your expectations of how God will respond to your questions or requests for help? What hope do you see in the way God answers Gideon?

7. The reflection above suggested that there are times when God tells us to stop waiting for the next answered prayer

and start acting on the last one. What was your last answered prayer? How have you acted on it?

8. God is often more likely to send an assignment than an answer. How do you respond? What is your next assignment?

9. How is God empowering you? For what purpose?

Focus for the Week

This week find three people in your inner circle—friends, family, coworkers, or others who know you well. Ask them to give you an honest answer to this question: "Do I take responsibility for my own stuff or have you noticed that I blame others?"

Prayer

Praise you, Lord! We praise you that your delays are for our own good. We honor you that your silence is for our blessing. We thank you that you are even waiting for us to act on the last answered to prayer that you sent before addressing this one. Thank you that all you do is for our good and our holiness. Amen.

Daily Scripture Readings

Monday: Judges 6:1-16
Tuesday: Judges 6:17-40
Wednesday: Judges 7:1-25
Thursday: Judges 8:22-27
Friday: Judges 8:28-35

4

APPEARANCES CAN BE DECEIVING

Gideon fashioned a priestly vest . . . and put it in his hometown of Ophrah. All Israel became unfaithful there because of it, and it became a trap for Gideon and his household.

(Judges 8:27)

I once heard about a guy who hit another man's empty, parked car in a crowded parking lot. Perhaps you've heard about or even seen a similar accident. Maybe you've even been there, done that! The "hitter" promptly got out of his car, leaned over the victim's car, and began to write a note. The note said, "Everyone looking at me right now thinks I'm leaving my name, insurance information, and phone number. I am not. Good luck."

Well, sir! For the sake of appearances, in order to look good, that guy ended up taking some of what didn't belong to him. He took some of the other driver's paint, plastic, and insurance policy. He took the money for the repairs that he should have been responsible for by departing the scene and leaving the other driver to foot the bill. And he did so in a deceptive manner that made it look as if he were doing the right thing. He protected his own reputation while emptying the other person's pockets, gaining at the expense of another in the sneakiest of ways.

You've probably done that at some level at one time or another. Hopefully you haven't done so as blatantly as the driver in the example above, but you've likely done something similar on a smaller scale. Maybe you've taken credit for things that you didn't do, for ideas that worked in spite of you and not because of you. I'm guilty of that. At Good Shepherd Church, we have an audio/visual team that creates videos, including sermon trailers, personal testimonies, and ministry promos. They combine art, wit, and technology, and I have to say they're *great*. And the people of the church tell me how great they are as well. And I usually respond with something like, "Ah, shucks, it was nothing. Just doing it for the Lord!" Except I'm not doing it at all! It really *is* nothing because nothing is what I contributed to it. I'm taking credit from the talented team who really did the work.

Perhaps you've done those things too. Maybe at work, you've gotten credit for a successful project, and yet the lion's share of the work came from one who is both underestimated and overlooked.

At school, perhaps someone else has done the study and you have gotten the benefit. Even in marriages and homes, I know some who take credit for things they didn't do. They're able to look good even when they've acted badly. I'd imagine that we've all done it at some point. You could say it's just part of survival; it's simply the way life goes.

Life's been going this way for quite a long time. In the last chapter, we studied the story of Gideon. Other than Samson, Gideon is the typically best-known of these not-very-well-known judges. Gideon is one whom God empowered to bring about a great victory over Midian. But his story doesn't stop there; it takes a turn for the worst. As we're going to see shortly, Gideon takes what doesn't belong to him by taking credit for something that he didn't do. It tarnishes his legacy and that of his family, and it leads Israel astray once again.

When we first meet Gideon in Judges 6, he is both tentative and halting before the Lord: "With all due respect, my Lord, how can I rescue Israel? My clan is the weakest in Manasseh, and I'm the youngest in my household" (Judges 6:15). By the time his story winds up in Judges 8, however, that demeanor has changed. It's like he's had a personality transplant. He has a dramatically increased confidence, due primarily to the ways God has used him to secure a series of military victories for the children of Israel. God worked through Gideon to fight and win against Israel's enemies, the Midianites, and Gideon pursued them until they were utterly defeated.

A critical element of Gideon's story is the emphasis on God's presence and power as the reason for the Israelites' victory, which is highlighted by Gideon's own reluctance to step up and lead. Remember, Gideon's first response to the angel who appears to him is to ask where God's mighty acts are (Judges 6:13). His second response is the one quoted above, where Gideon protests about his own weakness and youth (Judges 6:15). And despite the angel's reassurance, Gideon seeks signs to prove that God really is with him. First he asks for an opportunity to make an offering, which the angel consumes in dramatic, fiery fashion (Judges 6:18-23). Later, he asks for two signs involving fleece and dew, both of which occur exactly as Gideon requests (Judges 6:33-40). Gideon's hesitation, his own desire for reassurance of God's presence, shows that any victory will belong to God, not to Gideon or the people who fight with him.

The emphasis on God's power to bring about victory does not stop with Gideon's reluctance. When Gideon gathers the Israelites for battle, God specifically instructs the judge to send many of his men home:

> [2]The LORD said to Gideon: "You have too many people on your side. If I were to hand Midian over to them, the Israelites might claim credit for themselves rather than for me, thinking, We saved ourselves. [3]So now, announce in the people's hearing, 'Anyone who is afraid or unsteady may return home from Gideon's mountain.'" At this, twenty-two thousand people went home, and ten thousand were left.

> [4]The LORD said to Gideon, "There are still too many people. Take them down to the water, and I will weed them out for you there. Whenever I tell you, 'This one will go with you,' he should go with you; but whenever I tell you, 'This one won't go with you,' he should not go." [5]So he took the people down to the water. And the LORD said to Gideon, "Set aside those who lap the water with their tongues, as a dog laps, from those who bend

down on their knees to drink." ⁶The number of men who lapped was three hundred, and all the rest of the people bent down on their knees to drink water, with their hands to their mouths. ⁷Then the LORD said to Gideon, "With the three hundred men who lapped I will rescue you and hand over the Midianites to you. Let everyone else go home." ⁸So the people gathered their supplies and trumpets, and Gideon sent all the Israelites home, but kept the three hundred.

(Judges 7:2-8)

Gideon is about to attack the combined forces of the Midianites and the Amalekites, who are spread across a valley "like a swarm of locusts," with too many camels to count (Judges 7:12). And God tells Gideon to reduce his own army from thirty-two thousand down to three hundred, so the Israelites won't possibly be able to claim that they've won by their own strength. A victory of three hundred against a vast army will make it clear that God has been the one fighting for the Israelites. The implication is that neither the Israelites nor Gideon should boast or falsely take credit for the victory that ensues. Gideon should not make himself look good at God's expense.

THE VICTORY BELONGS TO GOD.

A dramatic victory does ensue. Gideon and his three hundred men rout the entire army of the Midianites and Amalekites, and Gideon pursues them until a total victory is won (Judges 7:8–8:21). And because of Gideon's reluctance to lead and his small army, it's clear that the victory belongs to God.

All that leads up to the closing scenes of Gideon's story at the end of Judges 8. The people approach Gideon and ask him to be a king over them. Here is the request from the people and Gideon's response:

> ²²Then the Israelites said to Gideon, "Rule over us, you and then your son and then your grandson, because you've rescued us from Midian's power."
>
> ²³Gideon replied to them, "I'm not the one who will rule over you, and my son won't rule over you either. The LORD rules over you." ²⁴But Gideon said to them, "May I make one request of you? Everyone give me the earrings from their loot"; the Midianites had worn gold earrings because they were Ishmaelites.
>
> ²⁵"We'll gladly give them," they replied. And they spread out a piece of cloth, and everyone pitched in the earrings from their loot. ²⁶The weight of the gold earrings that he requested was one thousand seven hundred shekels of gold, not counting the crescents, the pendants, and the purple robes worn by the Midianite kings, or the collars that were on their camels' necks. ²⁷Gideon fashioned a priestly vest out of it, and put it in his hometown of Ophrah. All Israel became unfaithful there because of it, and it became a trap for Gideon and his household.
>
> ²⁸So Midian was brought down before the Israelites and no longer raised its head. The land was peaceful for forty years during Gideon's time.
>
> (Judges 8:22-28)

The Israelites said to Gideon, "Rule over us, you and then your son and then your grandson, because you've rescued us from Midian's power" (verse 22). Note that wording: You, Gideon, have saved us from Midian. Actually, he didn't. God did. Gideon was a reluctant leader with only three hundred soldiers. And remember the warning not to boast, not to rob God of the credit: "You have too many people on your side. If I were to hand Midian over to them, the Israelites might claim credit for themselves rather than for me, thinking, We saved ourselves" (Judges 7:2). God has spoken these words to Gideon, so we expect that Gideon will correct the Israelites' mistake. We expect him to remind them that it was God, not he, who delivered Israel from Midian.

Except he doesn't. Look at Gideon's answer in verse 23: "I'm not the one who will rule over you, and my son won't rule over you either. The LORD rules over you." Now, that looks noble. It appears faithful; it appears humble. He is refusing the offer of kingship by saying that God is the true king. But for all the good appearance of Gideon's reply, the important thing is what it overlooks: he never corrects his countrymen's assertion that he has saved Israel from Midian. He never reminds them that deliverance came from God, not Gideon. In other words, he makes himself look good by stealing some of what legitimately belongs to God.

Look what happens next in 8:24: "But Gideon said to them, 'May I make one request of you? Everyone give me the earrings from their loot'; the Midianites had worn gold earrings because they were Ishmaelites."

I love this! *One more thing.* Like Columbo! Gideon asks for one more thing, one small request. And what is that one small request? He wants the gold earrings from the defeated Midianites. It's as if he doesn't want to be a king, but he sure wants to live like one. He doesn't want the pressure, but he does want the perks.

None of the burden, all of the bling. But notice what it is at the core of this loot: thievery. While he's making himself look good by declaring that the Lord is king, at the same time he steals from the conquered peoples. That's what plunder or loot is, after all: stuff you steal from people you have run out of town. And the Israelites' answer to this one teeny tiny request is to comply happily: "'We'll gladly give them,' they replied. And they spread out a piece of cloth, and everyone pitched in the earrings from their loot. The weight of the gold earrings that he requested was one thousand seven hundred shekels of gold, not counting the crescents, the pendants, and the purple robes worn by the Midianite kings, or the collars that were on their camels' necks" (Judges 8:25-26).

The Israelites answer, in other words, "We'd *love* to! You're our great leader; you're my boss. I'll do *anything* for you and do it with a smile!" And the result is a blanket full of bling for Gideon. First he has stolen credit, and now he's stolen gold—a lot of gold. One thousand seven hundred shekels would have been around 680 ounces, or 42 pounds of gold. To put that in perspective, in May 2017 gold traded at just over $1,200 per ounce. At that rate, all those gold earrings would've been valued at $816,000 in today's economy! Gideon's request is actually kind of masterful if appearances are what's most important.

But, of course, appearances *aren't* what's most important. And that's why everything next heads south.

Gideon took all this gold and fashioned it into a priestly vest: "Gideon fashioned a priestly vest out of it, and put it in his hometown of Ophrah. All Israel became unfaithful there because of it, and it became a trap for Gideon and his household" (Judges 8:27). In Hebrew, the garment is called an ephod. It sounds like a new product from Apple, or maybe something you ate for breakfast today, or the thing you're going to ride in to get to lunch. Biblical scholars aren't quite sure exactly what the ephod was or how it was worn in this case, but as the CEB translation indicates, it was most likely a priestly garment. In Exodus, Moses received instructions for creating an ephod that would be worn by the high priest when he ministered in the Tabernacle (Exodus 28:6-14; 39:2-7). And this one was made out of so much gold, I have to wonder if it looked like something Elvis or Liberace would have worn!

Now, the key is not what the garment was, exactly. The key is the effect that it had on the Israelites. As the second part of verse 27 says, "All Israel became unfaithful there because of it." In other words, the Israelites began using it to commit idolatry. Whatever it was, the priestly garment was so filled with gold that it immediately turned into an idol even with Gideon present. The people didn't wait till Gideon died to begin worshiping other gods. They did it while he was still alive, through the very item he created with the gold that he asked for.

First Gideon stole credit from God for victory over the Midianites. Then he stole the jewelry from the Midianites and others the Israelites defeated. And the result is a theft that's much, much worse—attention, glory, and worship stolen from God. That which belonged to God has been given to an idol, and if you know anything at all from the Old Testament, it's that idolatry is the one thing that makes God very, very angry. In Judges, it's idolatry that causes the oppression of the people by foreign powers time and time again. I don't know why they wanted to worship a gold lamé jacket, but they did!

Gideon's story concludes on a lamentable note, as the Israelites predictably fall back into idol worship after Gideon dies. As we have seen, it begins even while he was still alive, but it seems to become more widespread once Gideon is no longer on the scene.

Here is the rest of Judges 8, which tells of the end of Gideon's life and what happened afterwards.

> ²⁸So Midian was brought down before the Israelites and no longer raised its head. The land was peaceful for forty years during Gideon's time.
>
> ²⁹Jerubbaal, Joash's son, went home to live with his own household. ³⁰Gideon had seventy sons of his own because he had many wives. ³¹His secondary wife who was in Shechem also bore him a son, and he named him Abimelech. ³²Gideon, Joash's son, died at a good old age and was buried in the tomb of his father Joash in Ophrah of the Abiezrites.
>
> ³³Right after Gideon died, the Israelites once again acted unfaithfully by worshipping the Baals, setting up Baal-berith as their god. ³⁴The people of Israel didn't remember the LORD their God, who had delivered them from the power of all their enemies on every side. ³⁵Nor did they act loyally toward the household of Jerubbaal, that is, Gideon, in return for all the good that he had done on Israel's behalf.

Gideon's life was truly a mixed bag. What a military success. What a religious failure. What a military genius. What a religious poser. Do you see what he has lost in the progression through Judges 8? He's lost his honor, his reputation, his legacy—everything that has been important to him. The people at first wanted to make Gideon their king, but by the end of his story they are spitting on his grave! Gideon's progressive thefts lead to an aggressive loss. Here's the bottom line we can take away from the ignominious second half of Gideon's story: *When you take what doesn't belong to you, you lose what does.*

WHEN YOU TAKE WHAT DOESN'T BELONG TO YOU, YOU LOSE WHAT DOES.

Gideon took credit for victory, plunder from the enemy, and glory from God—none of which belonged to him—and in return he lost respect, integrity, and legacy. He was so concerned with keeping up his appearances that he completely lost face! The more he posed, the deeper he lost. *When you take what doesn't belong to you, you lose what does.*

How true this is. If we stop and think about it, we realize that we know the truth of this all too well. I've known people who have taken romantic partners that did not belong to them in acts of adultery. And in the aftermath of taking that, they lost what did belong to them: spouse, kids, home, church, reputation. Some have taken money or possessions that did not belong to them, and they have ended up losing their freedom as a result. Others have even taken safety from people on the road, and what they've lost is the ability to drive legally. If you do this kind of thing often enough at work or in school, you'll lose friends, you'll lose respect, you'll lose opportunity, and you may even lose that job.

You know where this is so applicable? With truth itself. The whole phenomenon of idolatry at the end of Gideon's story brings it home. One way to understand idolatry is to say that it's exchanging the truth of God for a lie. It's worshiping a golden priestly garment instead of the living God. It's worshiping any false god instead of the true God.

It's possible to steal truth, to replace it with a falsehood in your mind or in the minds of others, or even to rob people of the very

69

idea of truth so that they don't have anything concrete to hang onto. In the relatively recent history of the church, people have taken bits and pieces of the truth and quietly stolen it, bit by bit, from Scripture and from the Church. Deep truths—like the virgin birth of Jesus, the reality of heaven and hell, and the literal return of Jesus in glory—have been robbed of their power because we have tended to substitute lesser things for them, claiming that they're mere metaphors or ancient ideas that need to be modernized.

Teachers and writers, even pastors and theologians through the years have exchanged these truths for falsehoods and in the process have stolen what did not belong to them. The truth does not belong to us. Embodied in Scripture and the creeds, the truth is on loan to us. We are to hold it like a borrowed Stradivarius violin. "You be careful with this!" God is saying. "This is the faith passed once for all to the saints!" When we steal bits and pieces from this precious tapestry that's never been ours to begin with, the result is that we lose the church itself. We lose our own way, and become just another social enterprise. *When you take what doesn't belong to you, you lose what does.*

THE TRUTH IS ON LOAN TO US.

This is why I never use the phrase "my church" referring to the place where I serve as pastor. I never say that, or at least I try very hard to avoid saying that because it's not my church. The church belongs to Jesus Christ. I hope never to take what isn't mine because I don't want to lose what does belong to me. Confession time: it bothers me even when I hear other pastors mention the phrase "my church." The church I serve, any leadership position in the kingdom, is here on loan and I know how seriously God tasks us with faithful stewardship of these roles. And I know my heart and how deceitful it is, how much like Gideon I value appearances. So I know my own need for diligence. *When you take what doesn't belong to you, you lose what does.*

In a sense, it's a small thing, just my refusal to use a bit of shorthand in reference to the church I serve. But as Gideon's story shows, the smallest of things have the greatest of impact. It only took an army of three hundred men to rout the entire Midianite camp under Gideon's leadership. And it only took a succession of small thefts on Gideon's part to lead up to the great theft, idolatry, and the devastating personal loss that came as a result of it. All it took to get the ball rolling was a minor refusal to acknowledge God as the victor against Midian. Tiny honesties and minor deceptions alike can quickly grow in momentum and in influence.

It makes me think of an engineer who worked on developing the Boeing 747. He said the most satisfying moment of his life was when the first test flight launched. And what did he engineer on that massive plane? A switchbox about the size of a shoebox. Such a small piece of that massive plane. But tell me this: would you want it to be less than excellent when you're flying over the Atlantic? Faithfulness and excellence in small things lead up to success and favor in large things. And inattention, neglect, or faithlessness in small things can cause major problems down the road.

So let me ask you: are you honest in the small things? Are you faithful in sharing credit? Are you honest in giving generously? If you're married, do you guard your heart against unfaithfulness? If you're a small group leader, are you faithful in study and preparation so you don't casually and unknowingly rob the Gospel of some of its greatest treasures? In all of these examples and countless others, the stakes are unspeakably high. *When you take what doesn't belong to you, you lose what does.*

In Judges 8:31, we read about one of Gideon's many sons, the son of a concubine, named Abimelech. Abimelech's name is suggestive. It means "My father is king." Gideon, who declared to the Israelites that he would not be their king because that role belongs to God, has a son named "My father is king." Either Gideon or his concubine couldn't resist an opportunity to lend a royal air to their son despite Gideon's rejection of the kingship. And it's at this point that we realize something about Gideon: he has become the very thing he opposed. He ends up being the very thing he started out railing against. Early in his life, he is an idol breaker. Near the end, he is an idol maker. He started out avoiding becoming king but ended up claiming that status covertly in the name of his son. In all his gradual thievery, it turns out that the thing he lost the most was . . . himself. **When you take what doesn't belong to you, you lose what does.**

Questions for Reflection and Discussion

1. How concerned are you with appearances? When has your concern with how you look, or how others think about you, been counterproductive or outright harmful?

2. When have you taken credit for something that you didn't do, or that you didn't have very much to do with? What were the repercussions for you and the others involved?

3. Read back over Gideon's whole story in Judges 6–8. What changes do you notice within Gideon from beginning to end? How would you describe these changes, and what do you think brought them about?

4. Recall the whole story of Gideon and especially his legacy described in Judges 8:33-36. How does the arch of Gideon's life fit in the pattern of the Book of Judges?

5. What role do the Israelites who follow Gideon play in his story? How do they contribute to his downfall? What could they have done differently to result in a better outcome?

6. What does Gideon's story teach us about the need to be vigilant in our spiritual lives, especially after experiencing success in some form or another?

7. Recall something or someone you lost because of something or someone you took.

8. Name an area in your life where faithfulness in something small might be the precursor for an opportunity for faithfulness in something larger.

Focus for the Week

Chapter 1 of this book spoke of the importance of what we *inherit* in faith. And now chapter 4 repeats the same theme in slightly different language: be wary of stealing a portion of God's truth—a truth that belongs to the church and not to you. This will be the perfect week to declare (why simply recite when you can *declare*?) the Apostles' Creed. Do it together in your group. And do it every day as you prepare for the next group meeting. It will be a powerful reminder of the truths you steward on behalf of someone else.

Prayer

Lord Jesus, keep me diligent this week in things the world considers small or trivial. We know that you make no such distinctions. Keep me faithful, honest, and not at all territorial when it comes to what belongs to you. Amen.

Daily Scripture Readings

Monday: Judges 8:22-35
Tuesday: Judges 9:1-57
Wednesday: Psalm 1
Thursday: Psalm 24
Friday: Psalm 51

5

DÉJÀ VU ALL OVER AGAIN

Jephthah made a solemn promise to the LORD: "If you will decisively hand over the Ammonites to me, then whatever comes out the doors of my house to meet me when I return victorious from the Ammonites will be given over to the LORD. I will sacrifice it as an entirely burned offering" (Judges 11:30-31).

Remember William Shatner, the actor who played Captain Kirk of the U.S.S. Enterprise in the *Star Trek* movies and TV series? Well, his career has landed him in another recurring role: the Priceline Negotiator. He's a spokesperson for Priceline, a travel website that allows you to save money by booking hotels, flights, and other travel needs together. In this role, Shatner plays the smooth, confident, tough negotiator who uses Priceline to get outrageous deals for everyday people looking to travel. He's a negotiator with the stature of a bona fide superhero, a man who always gets the best rate. Always.

Secretly, most of us want to do at least some version of that expert negotiating. It's probably in my blood somewhere because my dad taught contracts in the law school at Southern Methodist University for thirty-one years. What are contracts if not the art of negotiation? People love that stuff. You may remember the glossy ads in airline magazines for Karrass Negotiating Seminars, short-term training sessions to help people improve their deal-making skills, and they're still offered today because people value the ability to negotiate well. The idea of strong negotiation experience and expertise was a key part of Donald Trump's presidential campaign—many people voted for him in part because of the expectation that he would become the de facto "Negotiator-in-Chief." He is certainly the first president ever with a book titled *The Art of the Deal*.

On a more personal level, the art of negotiation is why we like getting a good deal on a car. "Let me take this to my manager," the salesperson says. "This may get me in trouble, but I'll see what I can do." It makes us feel good about the price we are paying for the car, like we're getting a beneficial arrangement that isn't available to all. Others may like to negotiate compensation—which even happens in church, by the way. Still others have negotiated tough deals on their homes or other major purchases. And, sadly, some among us have had to negotiate through a divorce. Negotiation is tough, but in many cases it's something we enjoy. There's a back-and-forth dynamic, a give-and-take, a sense of timing and psychology.

And many of us think we're pretty good at it. We know we have bargaining chips in a given situation, and we like to use them to get the most out of it.

As we continue studying the Book of Judges, in this chapter we zero in on the character of Jephthah. And what we're going to discover is that Jephthah's story is all about negotiation. We find Jephthah's story in Judges 10–12, with the most interesting portion in Judges 11. To remind you where we are in Israel's history, Judges takes place approximately from 1200–1050 BC. It's after the Israelites enter the Promised Land under Joshua's leadership, and before the rise of the first kings, Saul and David. Judges tells the story of these years in a book of patterned history, in which ungoverned (and ungovernable) Israel keeps doing the same dumb things over and over again. The Israelites fall into deep collective sin, worshiping other gods instead of the one true God, and God allows them to be conquered and oppressed. Then they cry out to God, who sends them a deliverer (a judge), and under the judge's leadership, they return to peace and prosperity, living in faithfulness to God. But then they turn away from God again, and the same cycle starts over. Each new section in Judges is like déjà vu all over again!

The story of Jephthah is no exception. Like the ones before him, Jephthah's narrative begins with the Israelites turning away from God and worshiping others. Here's the description in Judges 10:6-9:

> ⁶Then the Israelites again did things that the LORD saw as evil. They served the Baals and the Astartes, as well as the gods of Aram, Sidon, Moab, the Ammonites, and the Philistines. They went away from the LORD and didn't serve him. ⁷The LORD became angry with Israel and handed them over to the Philistines and the Ammonites. ⁸Starting that year and for the next eighteen years, they

beat and bullied the Israelites, especially all the Israelites who lived on the east side of Jordan in the territory of the Ammonites in Gilead. ⁹The Ammonites also crossed the Jordan to make raids into Judah, Benjamin, and the households of Ephraim. So Israel was greatly distressed.

See? Déjà vu all over again! Just as the Israelites had done many times before, they again did what was evil and served other gods. This time, though, there's an interesting twist in the way it's described. The nature and the detail of Israel's sin are much more comprehensive here than elsewhere in Judges. The story specifically mentions *seven* groups of gods that the Israelites worshiped: the Baals and the Astartes, plus the gods of five separate people groups (Aram, Sidon, Moab, the Ammonites, and the Philistines). In the Bible, seven is the number of completion or perfection. By denoting seven groups of gods here, the author implies that the Israelites were being completely, perfectly disobedient.

What the Israelites were doing would be like if one Sunday I preached from the Quran instead of the Bible. And then the next Sunday our church leaders set up a palm reading for those attending worship. And the Sunday after that was a special Horoscope Sunday. And then the next week we prayed to a statue of the Buddha. In other words, it would be like if the church I served began worshiping Jesus *among* others instead of Jesus *alone*. In Judges 10, the Israelites were worshiping the Lord *among* others instead of the Lord *alone*. And they were doing it "better" and more comprehensively than ever before.

As a result, the Israelites experienced punishment just as they had each time before, with God removing divine protection and handing them over to their enemies. Déjà vu all over again. This time it's the Philistines and the Ammonites (Judges 10:7). Verse 8 tells us that the Philistines and Ammonites "beat and bullied" the

Israelites for eighteen years. The NIV translation uses the words "shattered and crushed." Israel's enemies shattered and crushed them. Complete, perfect disobedience leads to a crushing conquest. It's bad everywhere, but it's especially disastrous for the people across the Jordan, living in Gilead. That's where the Ammonites exerted their power most strongly.

After eighteen long years of this, the Israelites cry out to God just as they had in times past. This time, God doesn't deliver them right away. It takes some negotiation on the part of the Israelites.

> [10]Then the Israelites cried out to the LORD, "We've sinned against you, for we went away from our God and served the Baals."
>
> [11]The LORD replied to the Israelites, "When the Egyptians, Amorites, Ammonites, Philistines, [12]Sidonians, Amalekites, and Maonites oppressed you and you cried out to me, didn't I rescue you from their power? [13]But you have gone away from me and served other gods, so I won't rescue you anymore! [14]Go cry out to the gods you've chosen. Let them rescue you in the time of your distress."
>
> [15]The Israelites responded to the LORD, "We've sinned. Do to us whatever you see as right, but please save us this time." [16]They put away the foreign gods from among them and served the LORD. And the LORD could no longer stand to see Israel suffer.
>
> (Judges 10:10-16)

God's response to the Israelites suggests frustration, as if God knows that this time their repentance and outcry will be no more sincere or effective than they were in years past. It's like, *Weren't we just here? (yes) Didn't we do this before? (many times) Isn't this déjà vu all over again? (absolutely) Well, I'm done with that. Go let the gods you've been calling on liberate you.* God recalls saving the Israelites from the many nations who oppressed them (verse 12). Yet the Israelites have served other gods instead. So God says, "enough!" If Israel wants to serve other gods, then let those other gods bring salvation and deliverance (verses 13-14).

Perhaps you know something of what that's like for God or for Israel. Many people find themselves on one end or the other of a situation similar to this one. There's a pattern of sin that continues despite someone else's best efforts to help, offer support, or put a stop to it. It could take shape in many ways: alcohol, drugs, gambling, anger, or infidelity. And the person involved asks for help one too many times, and the other person or people finally say, enough. They get into Al Anon. They stop enabling or being codependent. They send a clear message: you got yourself into this mess. If you want to keep choosing alcohol, or drugs, or the thrill of gambling, then let these gods of yours get you out of it. It seems cruel at the time, but it's actually essential. If something doesn't change, the pattern just continues. I think that analogy helps us understand God's response to the Israelites. What we see in Judges 10 is an emotionally secure God, one who will not be a codependent enabler for the wayward people of Israel.

The people don't stop, though. They do their own version of the Negotiator in verses 15-16. They confess their sin and hand themselves over to God's mercy. "We've sinned. Do to us whatever you see as right, but please save us this time" (Judges 10:15). Then they stopped serving the other gods and began to serve the Lord alone. It looks like repentance, except we've seen this before. The Israelites aren't turning fully. They're *negotiating*. They're doing some give-and-take to bring about a desired outcome. "I was holding it for a friend. . . ." "I promise I'll never . . ." "If you will . . . , then I will . . ." Do whatever you want, God, just save us. See, we'll start worshiping you right now.

Shockingly, it works! Israel's words and actions, their see-right-through-it negotiation, elicit a response from God: "And the LORD could no longer stand to see Israel suffer" (Judges 10:16). On the surface, this looks like divine mercy. The Israelites' outcry and return to God tug at God's heartstrings just enough to make God want to save them. There's another way to translate God's words, though. The Hebrew is unclear. It could mean that God couldn't stand to see Israel suffer anymore. Or it could be translated as follows: "The LORD's soul/life became short/impatient with Israel's trouble."[4] In this sense, it conveys frustration, as if God had little confidence that the people would keep up with their end of the bargain. It's almost like God's saying, "I know this is probably not going to end well, but I will give you one more chance. And then I'll wash my hands of this mess." Because throughout this negotiation and the others that came before it, the people have only *wanted* God when they *needed* God. Of course, they're not the first and they're not the last. They have a knack for turning repentance into deal-making.

THE PEOPLE HAVE ONLY *WANTED* GOD WHEN THEY *NEEDED* GOD.

This knack for deal-making appears to give the Israelites some traction, because God apparently moves into action and arranges yet another military deliverer for them. This brings us to Jephthah, the deliverer God raises up. But we see from his intro at the beginning of Judges 11:1-3 that he is a different kind of cat:

¹Now Jephthah the Gileadite was a mighty warrior. Gilead was his father, but he was a prostitute's son. ²Gilead's wife gave birth to other sons for him, and when his wife's sons grew up, they drove Jephthah away. They told him, "You won't get an inheritance in our father's household because you're a different woman's son." ³So Jephthah ran away from his brothers and lived in the land of Tob. Worthless men gathered around Jephthah and became his posse.

How's that for the first line of a résumé? The son of a prostitute! He's a mighty warrior with questionable parentage, whose brothers drive him away because they don't want to share their inheritance with a prostitute's son. So Jephthah runs away and decides to head up a gang. In today's world, we know that family abandonment makes kids vulnerable to gangs. It's a sad reality of life in many places in the twenty-first century. Jephthah's experience proves that's nothing new; it was a sad reality in ancient Israel as well. But despite his misfortune, Jephthah remains a "mighty warrior." And with the Israelites in Gilead suffering at the hand of the Ammonites, Jephthah has a chance to do some negotiating of his own.

⁴Sometime afterward, the Ammonites made war against Israel. ⁵And when the Ammonites attacked Israel, Gilead's elders went to bring Jephthah back from the land of Tob. ⁶They said to him, "Come be our commander so we can fight against the Ammonites."

⁷But Jephthah replied to Gilead's elders, "Aren't you the ones who hated me and drove me away from my father's household? Why are you coming to me now when you're in trouble?"

⁸Gilead's elders answered Jephthah, "That may be, but now
we're turning back to you, so come with us and fight the
Ammonites. Then you'll become the leader over us and
everyone who lives in Gilead."

⁹And Jephthah said to Gilead's elders, "If you bring me
back to fight the Ammonites and the LORD gives them
over to me, I alone will be your leader."

¹⁰Gilead's elders replied to him, "The LORD is our witness;
we will surely do what you've said." ¹¹So Jephthah went
with Gilead's elders, and the people made him leader
and commander over them. At Mizpah before the LORD,
Jephthah repeated everything he had said.

(Judges 11:4-11)

Jephthah is a master negotiator. He's got bargaining chips. The
same people who disinherited him now need his protection, since
they know he's a mighty warrior and has organized a gang around
himself. "Why should I?" is his very logical reply. "Why should I
help those who exiled me?" The answer he gets is, "That may be,
but now we're turning back to you." In other words, "Help us just
because!" Which is not much of an answer.

Jephthah drives a hard bargain. He wisely and shrewdly notes
that the Israelites in Gilead have changed their offer. In 11:6, they
asked him to be their "commander." When he asks, "Why should
I help," they say he'll become their "leader" (11:8). It's a subtle
difference, but the word "leader" has the sense of something more
permanent, perhaps even with royal overtones. Jephthah makes a
counter-offer, saying that if he comes back to fight the Ammonites,
"I alone will be your leader" (11:9). The initial offer is commander,

but Jephthah negotiates his way to being the sole leader of all the Israelites in Gilead. Bravo! Now *that's* a Negotiator-in-Chief!

It's no surprise, then, that Jephthah begins his stint as Gilead's leader by attempting to negotiate with their conquerors. Jephthah's charge is to deliver his people from the Ammonites, so he first exchanges messages with the Ammonite king. The two go back and forth, with Jephthah asking why the Ammonites are making war in Gilead and the Ammonite king replying that their land rightfully belongs to his people. Jephthah, in turn, responds that the Israelites were given their land by the Lord, recounting the history of the Israelites' conquest as recorded in Numbers 20–22. We see that entire negotiation in Judges 11:12-28. Yet at the end of it all, Jephthah and the Ammonite king do not come to an agreement. "The Ammonite king refused to listen to the message that Jephthah sent to him" (Judges 11:28).

That means it's time for war, and here is where Jephthah trips up. Ensconced as a military leader, Jephthah prepares to go to battle. The Lord's spirit comes upon him, which all but ensures victory over the Ammonites (Judges 11:29). And then . . . Jephthah keeps negotiating. This time, he attempts to negotiate with God in an attempt to guarantee victory. In doing so, Jephthah asks for what he already has. And he makes a rash vow in an attempt to gain it, which has tragic consequences:

> [29]Then the LORD's spirit came on Jephthah. He passed through Gilead and Manasseh, then through Mizpah in Gilead, and from there he crossed over to the Ammonites. [30]Jephthah made a solemn promise to the LORD: "If you will decisively hand over the Ammonites to me, [31]then whatever comes out the doors of my house to meet me when I return victorious from the Ammonites will be given over to the LORD. I will sacrifice it as an entirely

burned offering." ³²Jephthah crossed over to fight the Ammonites, and the LORD handed them over to him. ³³It was an exceptionally great defeat; he defeated twenty towns from Aroer to the area of Minnith, and on as far as Abel-keramim. So the Ammonites were brought down before the Israelites.

³⁴But when Jephthah came to his house in Mizpah, it was his daughter who came out to meet him with tambourines and dancing! She was an only child; he had no other son or daughter except her. ³⁵When he saw her, he tore his clothes and said, "Oh no! My daughter! You have brought me to my knees! You are my agony! For I opened my mouth to the LORD, and I can't take it back."

(Judges 11:29-35)

Jephthah negotiates with God, attempts to manipulate God into granting him victory. A victory which, ironically, he could already count on because the Lord's spirit had come upon him. "If you . . . , then I . . . ," Jephthah says. If God brings about victory over the Ammonites, then Jephthah will sacrifice the first person (or animal) who comes out to meet him when he returns. If you . . . , then I . . . This is never a good way of relating to your Father. Never. It's almost like asking God for an answer and then deciding for yourself what the answer is. If you . . . , then I . . .

IF YOU . . . , THEN I . . .

Jephthah is not alone in that, is he? The truth is, many of us do it too. Jephthah is just more obvious about it than we are! But so many of us are guilty of relating to God in that way somehow. If you . . . , then I . . . If you save my life, I'll never miss church again. If you rescue my marriage, I'll start tithing. If you demolish these urges within me, I'll become a missionary. If you heal my child, then I'll get more involved in service and ministry. We try to manipulate God, negotiate with God, offer God things in order to get God to do what we want. We choose to wheel and deal with God instead of trusting and having a relationship with God. If you . . . , then I . . .

In this particular negotiation with Jephthah, God does not answer back. In fact, God's silence in response to the vow and in what happens next is deafening (if you remember, we saw that same pattern in chapter 1 of this book. Judges tells history more *in patterns* than *with precision*). God grants victory to Jephthah, and it results in an "exceptionally great defeat" that brings down Ammonites (Judges 11:32-33). And then Jephthah goes home, and his own daughter is the first to come out to greet him—dancing and playing tambourines just like Israelite women did in celebration of victory. Jephthah tears his clothes in grief because of his vow and because he would now have to sacrifice her. "I opened my mouth to the LORD," Jephthah says in anguish, "and I can't take it back" (Judges 11:35).

Which is actually *wrong*. The gods of other nations—remember those the Israelites had worshiped—might have allowed child sacrifice and held their people to obscene vows. But not the Lord. God didn't allow child sacrifice, never wanted it. See, when you misunderstand God as one who negotiates, you misunderstand a whole lot else about God as well. Jephthah thought there was no way out other than giving to God his only daughter. In verses 36-40, we see what happened to her.

> [36]But she replied to him, "My father, you've opened your mouth to the LORD, so you should do to me just what

you've promised. After all, the LORD has carried out just punishment for you on your enemies the Ammonites." [37]Then she said to her father, "Let this one thing be done for me: hold off for two months and let me and my friends wander the hills in sadness, crying over the fact that I never had children."

[38]"Go," he responded, and he sent her away for two months. She and her friends walked on the hills and cried because she would never have children.

[39]When two months had passed, she returned to her father, and he did to her what he had promised. She had not known a man intimately. But she gave rise to a tradition in Israel where [40]for four days every year Israelite daughters would go away to recount the story of the Gileadite Jephthah's daughter.

The result of this is a little ambiguous. Did Jephthah slay his daughter? Or did he fulfill his vow by setting her apart as a perpetual virgin? We don't know for sure, though most readers have thought through the years that he did in fact offer her life as a sacrifice. If he did slay her, why did God not intervene like with Abraham's near-sacrifice of Isaac (Genesis 22)? We can't be certain. But when God is silent in a narrative like this, one possibility is that God is leaving people to their own devices. God might be allowing Jephthah and those around him to reap their own consequences.

It's so tragic. Jephthah could have had a great legacy! He was a winning warrior, empowered by God's spirit. He'd negotiated a prominent leadership role. But no! Just like with Gideon, he undermined his own success and left a legacy and reputation that are decidedly mixed. The patterns of personal failure repeat for Israel's judges just as the patterns of sin repeat for Israel! Déjà vu all over again. It's all headed toward everyone doing right in their own eyes, as we explored in the first chapter. In Jephthah's case, he is chained by his heritage (questionable parentage), shackled by his disinheritance, and burdened by his ignorance of the character of God. He's made it through life via shrewd negotiation, and he fatally attempts the same thing with God. And his own daughter bears the consequences. When we negotiate as a default, the people closest to us pay the price. But God seeks something else, something better for us. *God doesn't want to negotiate. God wants to liberate.*

GOD DOESN'T WANT TO NEGOTIATE. GOD WANTS TO LIBERATE.

God didn't want to make deals with Jephthah. God wanted to empower him and deliver him! God wanted to liberate him from his past, from his rage, from his ignorance. And Jephthah, as a crash test dummy, can't quite do it. He's got so much scar tissue from life that he doesn't trust anything but himself. He thinks God is just one more god, one more person with whom he can drive a hard bargain. But *God doesn't want to negotiate. God wants to liberate.*

If someone needs to be liberated from alcohol, the answer is not "If you . . . , then I . . ." The answer is "Because you . . . , I am. . ." Because you are holy, I am serene! Because you are God, I am free! Healing and liberation come from God's character, not from our performance. If someone needs to be liberated from a lifetime pattern of dishonesty—lying and getting into stuff and then lying to get out of stuff—the answer is not "If you . . . , then I . . ." No! Because you are Truth, I am now truthful. It comes from God's character, not your performance. Like with casual faith. "If you make it convenient, then I'll go to church." "If the music's good, the sermon's interesting, the people are pretty, then I will commit." No! Because you are the Great I AM, I am a worshiper. *God doesn't want to negotiate. God wants to liberate.*

And here's a dirty little secret. God can't really liberate you until God is your one and only. When you *want* God only when you *need* him, you'll find you need God all the time because you keep tripping up. When you confuse repentance with negotiation, God might just leave you to your own devices. It will be déjà vu all over again, and like Jephthah, the results won't be pretty.

There is a beautiful continuity between the testaments here. How does Jesus word it in Luke 4? "He has sent me to preach good news to the poor, to proclaim release to the prisoners . . . and to proclaim the year of the Lord's favor" (Luke 4:18-19). How does Paul reinforce it in Galatians 5? "Christ has set us free for freedom" (Galatians 5:1). The thread is continuous and invigorating: your life and your salvation do not depend on your performance for Jesus but instead on your position in Jesus. Why try to negotiate for what is already yours?

Oh lay your expert negotiation down. Let God be your one and only. Only then can God truly emancipate you. Because I want my legacy and your legacy to be free of ambiguity and full of holiness. No more crash test dummies. No more déjà vu all over again. No more Jephthahs. *God doesn't want to negotiate. God wants to liberate.*

Questions for Reflection and Discussion

1. When it comes to buying a car, setting a salary, or even bartering for goods in an open-air bazaar, how do you rate your negotiating skills?

2. When have you been on the receiving end of someone else's negotiating skill? How did you feel at the end?

3. When have you tried to make a "deal" with God, or been tempted to do so? How did it turn out?

4. From the reflection above and the text of Judges 10–12, list all the things that have imprisoned Jephthah.

5. What opportunities to be free does Jephthah have? How does he take advantage of them, and how does he miss them?

6. What do you make of God's silence in response to Jephthah's vow, and of his fulfillment of the vow? What does the silence say about God?

7. What difference would it have made for Jephthah to trust that God's spirit was on him and that it would ensure victory? Did Jephthah lack trust in God, or trust in himself?

8. What will it mean for you to allow the Lord to be your one and only?

Focus for the Week

Because so much of Jephthah's story revolves around the notion that "we want God only when we need God," try a prayer experiment this week: *intercede for others rather than pleading for yourself.* To clarify, it is not a sin, nor is it selfish, to pray for yourself. However, for this next week, you might discover unusual freedom in praying exclusively for the needs of others.

Prayer

Lord Jesus, thank you that you are the freedom giver. Thank you that you don't relate to me on the basis of what I negotiate with you. I give you my life, my heart, my all. I honor you this week for the

fact that we can sing "In Christ Alone" and not "In Christ Among."
Amen!

Daily Scripture Readings

Monday: Philippians 2:1-11
Tuesday: Luke 9:57-62
Wednesday: Mark 8:27-38
Thursday: Colossians 1:15-20
Friday: Matthew 4:18-22

6

THE GAP YEARS

"He'll be the one who begins Israel's rescue from the
power of the Philistines."

(Judges 13:5)

There is a gap between the Samson we think we know and the
Samson we find in Scripture. In the world of the Bible, church,
Jesus, and faith, there are many such gaps—spaces of distance
between popular conception and what we actually find in the Bible.
And the gap between the Samson of popular imagination and
the Samson of the Book of Judges is one of the most interesting

gaps I know of. It's the distance between the Samson we *want* and the Samson we *get*. It's the gap, really, between the Samson of folklore and the Samson of the Bible. Or between the Samson of my illustrated children's Bible and the Samson we really find in the pages of the Book of Judges.

Many of us know a little something about Samson. Whether we're churchgoers or not, regular Bible readers or not, we know a few key pieces of the story. You probably know already, for instance, that his female companion is Delilah. You probably know that he's really strong. And you probably know that the source of his strength is his really long hair. In popular imagination, Samson is the guy with Delilah. The guy with the guns. The guy with the hair. In other words, he's a cross between Fabio and Dr. McDreamy. And we probably know that Delilah somehow betrayed him, cut off his hair, and took away his strength.

And yet as we open up Samson's story in Judges 13–16, we see quickly that Samson's life is much more tragic and much more complicated than what we hear about him. If the Book of Judges is a story of Israel as crash test dummies, we might say that Samson is probably the crash test dumbest of them all. There's a major gap between the Samson of our children's Bibles and the Samson of Judges. And not only is there a gap between the Samson of folklore and the Samson of Scripture, but more critically there's a gap between who Samson *could have been* and who he *was*.

Throughout this book, we've been studying the Book of Judges with the understanding that the Israelites act like crash test dummies: they strap themselves into a car and slam headlong into a brick wall. And then they do it again. And again. And again. They fall into patterns of sin, repeating their acts of unfaithfulness to God throughout the book with the same tragic consequences every time. The period of the judges, about 1200–1050 BC, was a time in which the Israelites were both ungoverned and ungovernable. And the book itself is this series of recurring cycles and repeating patterns in which the people of God keep doing the same things over and over again with mind-numbing stupidity. And they never learn! In fact, the level of chicanery and depravity escalate as the book goes on. The later cycles in the book are worse than the first! The text culminates with self-centered anarchy in 21:25, the last sentence of the book that perfectly summarizes all that has come before it: "In those days there was no king in Israel; each person did what they thought to be right" (Judges 21:25).

Within this context, Samson emerges as the apex (or rock bottom) of those cycles. Rather than the hero many of us have understood him to be, Samson is actually the embodiment of the anarchy and self-centeredness that define the entire Israelite people by the end of Judges. We'll see how this is true by looking at some snapshots of his life, the story that's told in Judges 13–16. A fascinating pattern emerges in those snapshots. As we explore Samson's story, we'll discover how we can avoid falling into the same traps that he did.

Samson's story begins much the same way as the other narratives of the judges before him. At the start of the story we read: "The Israelites again did things that the LORD saw as evil, and he handed them over to the Philistines for forty years" (Judges 13:1). Now if you're like me, you're asking, "Wait, haven't I read this before?" And the answer is yes, yes you have. It's all over the book! That's why the Israelites in Judges are crash test dummies. Each new cycle begins the same way as the ones before it. What will be different in this one is the nature of the judge, the deliverer, Samson.

The second verse of Judges 13 tells us of Samson's birth. Samson's birth is interesting because it's almost like Jesus' birth. In fact, it's similar to other miraculous births in Scripture, including the birth of Isaac to Abraham and Sarah. The story involves an angel who appears to Samson's mother, the promise of a miraculous birth, and a child who will be marked from birth for a special purpose. The full account is in Judges 13:2-24. I won't quote the full Scripture passage here. But I do want to point out that the angel gives Samson's mother specific instructions about how to dedicate the child as a Nazarite, someone who would be set apart for special service to God. Samson will be a Nazarite his whole life, which will mean that his hair won't be cut and that he is to avoid not only alcohol but everything that the Scripture declares unclean (Judges 13:2-5; see Numbers 6:1-21). That's why Samson's long hair is considered the source of his strength.

At the end of Judges 13, Samson is born and his mother names him (Judges 13:24). The name *Samson* comes from the Hebrew word for sun, so his name may mean something like "Sun Child" or "Bright Sun." The hopeful name, combined with the angel's words to Samson's parents, heighten the expectations of what this particular judge is going to be and do. Samson has hope and light attached to him. As he grows up, we read that "the LORD blessed him" and "the LORD's spirit began to move in him" (Judges 13:24-25). Which makes the subsequent crash to earth that much more painful.

Speaking of which, look at the beginning of Judges 14. The crash begins almost with Samson's first recorded acts as an adult.

> [1]Samson traveled down to Timnah. While he was in Timnah, a Philistine woman caught his eye. [2]He went back home and told his father and mother, "A Philistine woman in Timnah caught my eye; now get her for me as a wife!"
>
> [3]But his father and mother replied to him, "Is there no woman among your own relatives or among all our people

that you have to go get a wife from the uncircumcised Philistines?"

Yet Samson said to his father, "Get her for me, because she's the one I want!"

(Judges 14:1-3)

Samson sees a woman he wants and decides to marry her even though she's a Philistine, one of Israel's enemies. He sees, he wants, he gets. In verse 3, when he says "she's the one I want," a literal translation of Samson's words is "she's right in my eyes." It echoes the language at the end of Judges, in which every person does what is right in their own eyes (Judges 21:25). The gap between Samson's impulse and his action is microscopic. He has an impulse, and he acts on it almost right away. And that impulsive behavior rapidly gets him into further trouble.

Later Samson goes to marry the Philistine woman, and as part of the wedding festivities, he strikes a bet with the young Philistine men of the city. He tells them a riddle, and if they can answer the riddle within seven days, he'll give them thirty sets of garments. But if they can't answer it, they have to give him thirty sets of garments. The men find the answer to the riddle by threatening Samson's bride and her father, and she persuades Samson to tell her the answer (Judges 14:10-18). When Samson realizes what the young men have done, he becomes angry. He pays the wager by acquiring thirty garments through violence:

> [19]Then the LORD's spirit rushed over him, and he went down to Ashkelon. He killed thirty of their men, stripped them of their gear, and gave the sets of clothes to the ones who had told the answer to the riddle. In anger, he went

back up to his father's household. ²⁰And Samson's wife married one of those who had been his companions.

(Judges 14:19-20)

Samson commits mass murder and then leaves his wife in anger. He discards her like an obsolete cassette. Notice again: there's no gap between his impulse and his actions. There is no distance between having an appetite and satisfying it. He becomes angry, and then he goes on a rampage and uses his impressive strength to kill thirty men. As if that isn't enough, he eventually returns to his wife but becomes enraged again when he discovers that she's been given to another man (Judges 15:2-3). He takes revenge by capturing foxes, tying torches to their tails, and turning them loose among the grain, vineyards, and orchards of the Philistines (15:4-5). The Philistines, in turn, react by burning Samson's wife and her father to death (15:6). That part was conveniently left out of my childhood Bible story book about Samson! Samson's understandable response is in Judges 15:7-8:

> ⁷Samson then responded to them, "If this is how you act, then I won't stop until I get revenge on you!" ⁸He struck them hard, taking their legs right out from under them. Then he traveled down and stayed in a cave in the rock at Etam.

The NIV translates the first part of verse 8 as "He attacked them viciously and slaughtered many of them." The child of the sun brings about a lot of darkness, does he not?

When you read this pile-on of events, Samson seems like an animal, doesn't he? He comes across as an impulsive, immensely strong brute. He reminds me somewhat of our family cat. She's a sweet animal. She loves us. But when we're on the back porch, and she is loving us, sometimes she will hear a bird. Immediately there's a jolt, and she suddenly focuses only on locating and hunting that bird. Instinct takes over. There is no gap between her hearing the bird and acting on it. Killing a bird is a stronger impulse for a cat than loving a human. That's what Samson is like. He has no gap between having an impulse and acting on it. His life philosophy seems to be summarized in Judges 15:11, when he explains to his people why he attacked the Philistines: "I did to them just what they did to me." It's the anti-Golden Rule. It's revenge, paying back evil for evil. Samson's birth story might be reminiscent of Jesus, but nothing else about him is.

Samson's impulsive behavior continues in the next chapter, when he visits a prostitute in the Philistine city of Gaza. The Philistines attempt to trap him in the city, but Samson uses his superhuman strength to tear down the doors of the city gates and escape (Judges 16:1-3). It's another story that was left out my illustrated children's Bible. But notice again: He saw, he wanted, he got. There's no hesitation, no reflection, no counting the cost. It's all appetite, all instinct, all impulse. Remember: this is a guy marked by God! He's been set apart by a special vow. His birth story suggested greatness. But he falls far short. He's broken his vow by touching corpses and drinking alcohol. And he's acted violently and impulsively. He uses his great strength to inflict brutal violence or to save himself from disasters of his own making. The gap between Samson's impulse and his action vanished a long time ago. As a result, the gap between his *potential* and his *actual* is enormous. He could be so great, but he doesn't live up to his potential.

All that is why Samson's entanglement with Delilah—the part of the story we're familiar with—ends predictably. He falls in love with her, and the Philistine leaders pay her an enormous sum to find out the secret of his strength. Every time she asks, he lies to her, but she eventually wears him down. He tells her the truth, that he's been a Nazarite from childhood and that his hair has never been cut. She betrays him, and the Philistines capture him and gouge out his eyes. No more seeing, wanting, and getting for Samson! It's a tragic irony: the man who *did right in his own eyes* now has no eyes to see with. His impulsive behavior has brought him to rock bottom, and with his hair cut short, he doesn't have the strength to get out of it this time.

Eventually, though, Samson's hair grows back while he's imprisoned by the Philistines. They hold a celebration to their god because they've captured Samson, and they bring him into the god's temple to perform in front of them. He's reduced to the level of a carnival act. Samson's strength returns, and he performs one final act of revenge against the Philistines:

> [26]Samson said to the young man who led him by the hand, "Put me where I can feel the pillars that hold up the temple, so I can lean on them." [27]Now the temple was filled with men and women. All the rulers of the Philistines were there, and about three thousand more men and women were on the roof watching as Samson performed. [28]Then Samson called out to the LORD, "LORD God, please remember me! Make me strong just this once more, God, so I can have revenge on the Philistines, just one act of revenge for my two eyes." [29]Samson grabbed the two central pillars that held up the temple. He leaned against one with his right hand and the other with his left. [30]And Samson said, "Let me die with the Philistines!" He strained with all his might, and the temple collapsed on the rulers and all the people who were in it. So it turned

out that he killed more people in his death than he did during his life.

(Judges 16:26-30)

The bloodshed and violence at Samson's hands are tremendous. There are thirty murdered men; a burned wife and father-in-law; vandalized fields; more murdered Philistines; and now the Philistine leaders and three thousand others dead in the destruction of their temple. Samson's other moral failures include visiting a prostitute, discarding his wife, and neglecting his Nazarite vow. At the end of his life, we see all the factors piling up one after another—women, revenge, strength—and it all comes crashing down on Samson in a heap of rubble. He is trapped, imprisoned, dead along with his enemies. I can't help but think about what might have been if he'd taken a different course. Think of all he *could have done* lined up against all he *did*. There's such a gap.

Samson had a huge gap between his potential and his actual because he had almost no gap at all between his impulses and his actions. He's not the only one, not the last one, for which this is true. Samson is hardly the last one to surrender to his impulses. I've participated in it. I've observed it. I will long remember that time, very early in my ministry career, when there was a family I just knew I needed to visit so that I could set them straight about some things in the church. My wife Julie warned me not to go. But I knew better. She pleaded with me not to go. But I knew better! I had an impulse to get the last word in, to be a know-it-all with this unsuspecting family, so I forged ahead. And the fallout? Well, I didn't end up as a blinded carnival act stranded in a heap of rubble . . . but it remains one of my most difficult seasons of full-time ministry. All because I had an impulse and I surrendered to it.

So I've participated. And I've observed. One of the saddest notes I've seen was an apology written by a young man to the father of the young woman he had impregnated. Innocence ended, plans uprooted, lives altered all because of surrendering to impulses.

Many of us are mini-Samsons, not because we have long hair, or because we are strong, or because we use foxes and fire creatively. We are mini-Samsons because we routinely surrender to our impulses and end up imprisoned by the consequences. There is no gap between what we think and what we say, between what we feel and what we do.

Now, you think I'm going straight into sex, booze, and drugs to describe these impulses and their consequences. And yes, it certainly applies in all those instances. But there's more. Impulse control, or lack of it, bears on much more of life than we realize. For some, it may be road rage. Someone passes you on the right, cuts you off, and causes you to blow a fuse in traffic. Your impulse is to yell at the other driver, to honk, to give him half the peace sign. And it only takes one time for those impulses to escalate out of control. Then all of a sudden, because of an inability to grow the gap between impulse and action, there's a mess. People hurt and property damaged. Police involved. All it takes is one time for things to go really wrong.

For others, it may be the impulse to be right. You have such an appetite for correction that you'll even correct the wrong people (like your boss) in the wrong setting (in public). And you wonder why there's no promotion! Or you give in to that desire to be right too often around your loved ones, and your relationships suffer because of it. Or maybe it's the impulse to buy. To purchase. Like Samson, you see, you want, you get. You didn't know the product even existed until you saw it, but once you saw it, you couldn't live without it—even if you had to go into debt to get there.

In each of these instances and many more, there's no gap between our impulse and our action. And because of that, there's a big gap between who we are and who we could be. Each time we give in to those harmful impulses rather than resisting them, we settle for a little bit less out of life. We choose something a little bit lower than our full potential. In Samson's case, it all added up over a lifetime to disappointing, tragic results.

You know what your impulse is. You know where and how it is that you repeatedly surrender to that impulse. And each time you do, there you go again, being a crash test dummy just like Samson and the Israelites. So, how do we stop being crash test dummies? How do we make sure we don't become like Samson, dead in the middle of the rubble that we caused? How can we avoid God needing to work in spite of us, rather than inside of and through us? How can we become God's partner rather than God's obstacle?

THE KEY IS TO TURN OUR WILL, LIVES, IMPULSES, AND EMOTIONS OVER TO GOD.

Here's where our friends in recovery from addiction live the gospel whether they know it or not. Steps two and three of the twelve-step Alcoholics Anonymous recovery program involve acknowledging that only a Higher Power (we call him Jesus, the Highest Power!) can restore one to sanity. They also involve a decision to turn one's will and life over to God's care, as God is understood. In other words, the key is to turn our will, lives, impulses, and emotions over to God. Daily. Hourly. Repeatedly. It's one moment of surrender followed by a million other moments of surrender. It's where we acknowledge that if we don't surrender this impulse to God, we're going to have to surrender to it. And whatever it is (drinking, shopping, arguing, anger), it will imprison us. So here's the key. Here's what Samson could never do, and what I long for us to be able to do: *Surrender your impulses so you don't surrender to them.* Those are our choices. Surrender those impulses to God, acknowledging that we are powerless, or surrender to those very impulses and all their nasty consequences.

When we surrender those impulses to God, I'm convinced that the most amazing thing happens: the gap between our impulses and our actions grows. Because we surrender, we're no longer governed by our appetites. We govern them instead. And God does it. God restores the sanity, grows the gap. What I mean is, the more we surrender those impulses, the greater control we will discover we have. The less power those impulses will have over us. It takes time, patience, and perseverance. But by the grace of God, it happens. Instead of giving the finger on the road, you breathe, pause, and realize you'll get to your destination more quickly without the conflict. God does it. You see an ad online or a display at the store and you realize: if I resist, I can give. And God does it. And you are tempted toward an unhealthy relationship, and then the words of my friend and fellow author Chris Ritter come to mind: I want "to join the passionate ranks of the sexually restrained."[5] And God does it. *Surrender your impulses so you don't surrender to them.*

SURRENDER YOUR IMPULSES SO YOU DON'T SURRENDER TO THEM.

Can I confess one area where this brings up some uncertainty? The medical conditions known as ADD and ADHD, Attention Deficit Disorder and Attention Deficit Hyperactivity Disorder. These conditions have at their core a lack of impulse control. I've seen situations where medicine seemed to help, and I've seen situations where medicine seemed to hurt. I know many people had a hard time because they grew up before we were aware of these conditions. And I know that others have grown up in a time when these conditions have been over-diagnosed, which causes a different sort of difficulty. So there's uncertainty there. But I will say this: I always trust that God's power works even over our brain chemistry, even alongside Ritalin or other medications. Medications can even be vehicles for God's power to work. *Surrender your impulses so you don't surrender to them.*

A friend of mine from Liberia once showed me a great example of impulse control. He's a friend from Good Shepherd, where I serve as pastor, and the incident was an eye-opener. We have a ministry at Good Shepherd blessing houses in our surrounding neighborhoods. One day, this friend and I were out blessing houses, and as we met people in their homes, I introduced us and explained why we were there. With each new person we met, I kept saying that my friend was from Ghana. Except he's from Liberia, and I've known that forever. He just stood and smiled, every time. But eventually, after my third time of misidentifying his country of origin, we got in the car and he confronted me about it. "Pastor, I'm from Liberia, not Ghana," he said. And then he went on to say, "When I was a younger man, I would have corrected you in front of those people. But now that I'm older, I know better. But *don't* get it wrong again!" He showed restraint, he controlled his impulse even though he would have been fully justified in correcting me in front of others. And I received a blessing as a result. *Surrender your impulses so you don't surrender to them.*

I received a similar lesson from a fellow pastor once. Speaking to a group of clergy, he told us, "Whenever you want to get the last word in, don't." Inwardly, I protested. I have so many last words! But *don't*. I knew he was right. The benefits of restraint far outweigh the impulse to launch whatever zinger comes to mind. So by and large, I don't get the last word in. And my relationships have benefited from it. *Surrender your impulses so you don't surrender to them.*

I'd like to end with a story of a recovering alcoholic who experienced a miracle when he surrendered his impulse to God. A fellow pilgrim asked him if he really believed that Jesus turned water into wine. He replied simply, "I don't know about that. All I know is that in my house he turned beer into furniture." *Surrender your impulses so you don't surrender to them.* And it's the real story of Samson that shows us how it comes to pass.

Questions for Reflection and Discussion

1. Think through what you know of Samson from popular imagination. What is that version of Samson like?

2. Based on the reflection above and your reading of Judges 13–16, how would you characterize the Samson of the Bible? In what ways is he different from the Samson we usually think of?

3. How do you explain the gap between the Samson of folklore and the Samson who is really in Scripture?

4. Is Samson's violence justified? Why or why not?

5. What could Samson's life and legacy have been like if he'd controlled his impulses better? What in the biblical text suggests this?

6. In the space below, jot down some areas of your life where you struggle controlling your impulses.

7. Recall a time or times when a lack of self-control has gotten you in trouble—whether at school, at work, in your family, or with your faith.

8. Who in your experience has successfully surrendered their impulses to God? What difference has it made in their lives?

Focus for the Week

A white flag is a traditional symbol of surrender. Take a few moments and listen to the song "White Flag" by Chris Tomlin (a link to the video is available at https://www.youtube.com/watch?v=Lk8ue3qN0hg). On a small sheet of paper, draw a simple picture of a white flag. Carry it in your pocket through the coming week as an indication and reminder of your surrendered impulses.

Prayer

Heavenly God, we surrender all. Not some. Not most. ALL. We especially surrender our impulses. Purify them and protect us from the enemy we see in the mirror. Thank you for the gift of holiness. Amen.

Daily Scripture Readings

Monday: Galatians 5:22-23
Tuesday: 1 Thessalonians 4:1-12
Wednesday: 2 Peter 1:1-11
Thursday: Titus 2:1-15
Friday: 1 Corinthians 6

NOTES

Chapter 1

1. John Irving, *A Prayer for Owen Meany* (New York: William Morrow, 2013; reprint, New York: William Morrow, 1989), 627.

2. "Nothing but the Blood," *The United Methodist Hymnal* (Nashville: The United Methodist Publishing House, 1989), 362.

3. Adapted from The Apostles' Creed, *United Methodist Hymnal* 881.

Chapter 2

4. *The CEB Study Bible with Apocrypha* (Common English Bible, 2013), 388 OT.

Chapter 4

5. Chris Ritter, "The Wrong Side of History," *People Need Jesus: Leading Toward a Jesus-Focused Church* (blog), February 17, 2015, https://peopleneedjesus.net/2015/02/17/the-wrong-side -of-history/. Accessed July 21, 2017.

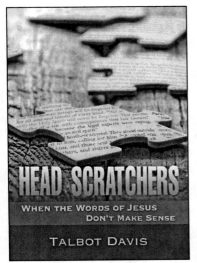

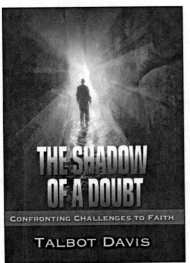

CPSIA information can be obtained
at www.ICGtesting.com
Printed in the USA
FSOW02n2347250917
39147FS